TRAINS AROUND THE WORLD

contents page

Giant engine's trial trip, 1 October 1926: the most powerful passenger engine at that time in the British Isles, Southern Railway's *Lord Nelson* leaving Waterloo.

front endpaper

Reading's Nos. 2100 and 2102 with an excursion train bound for West Milton, Pennsylvania from Philadelphia.

back endpaper

A 2–6–0 Mogul type locomotive, built by Alco in 1909 on the East Jordan & Southern Railway No. 6.

TRAINS AROUND THE WORLD

First published 1972 by
Octopus Books Limited,
59 Grosvenor Street, London W1

© 1972 Octopus Books Limited
Reprinted 1973
ISBN 0 7064 0078 X
Filmset by «Les Presses Saint-Augustin», Bruges, Belgium

Produced by Mandarin Publishers Limited
77ᵤ Marble Road, North Point, Hong Kong
Printed in Hong Kong

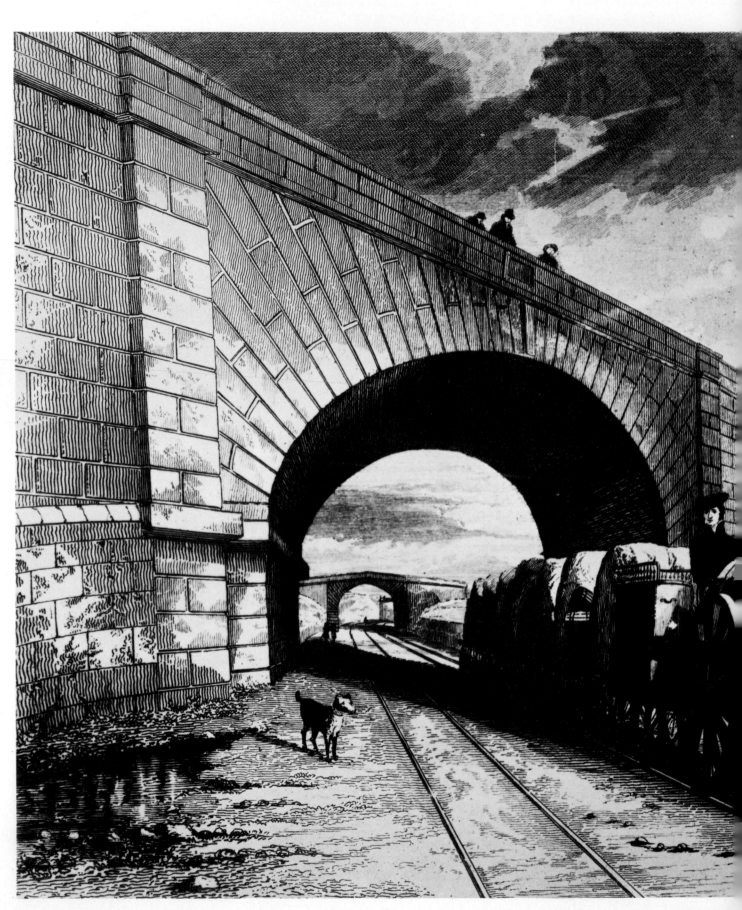

Perhaps no locomotive ever built has greater claim to fame than Stephenson's *Rocket*, and indeed there can be few people who have not heard of this notable, early steam engine. And yet few realize the real reasons for its fame; that it represented the first breakthrough from a prolonged period of trial and error invention to establish once and for all the potential efficiency of steam locomotion.

Prior to the design of *Rocket* a number of creative engineers had applied their talents to the possibilities of a steam-powered replacement of the faithful horse as a means of wagon haulage upon the special tracks, or tramroads, laid down in mines. These tracks had existed in various primitive forms for more than two centuries, both on the Continent and in Great Britain, and the British wagon-ways had been further developed to link the mines with staithes or wharfs, where barges and coastal craft were loaded for shipment. The actual design of rail and wheel varied somewhat and this aspect was to prove something of an 'Achilles heel' to the development of early steam locomotives.

It was Richard Trevithick – sometimes described as the Father of the Locomotive – who first developed high-pressure, stationary engines as against the low-pressure of the cumbersome pumping engines in use at the beginning of the nineteenth century. He was persuaded to build a steam locomotive adaptation of his high-pressure, stationary engines then being installed at the Pen-y-darran ironworks, near Merthyr Tydfil, Wales, for use on their works tramway, which was then served by horses. First tried out on 13 February 1804, this original locomotive had a single, horizontal cylinder located within the boiler, driving a cranked shaft with an enormous flywheel by means of a cross-head on long, projecting slidebars. Basically, it was his stationary engine adapted to make it move along, with the power transmitted to the axles through spur wheels. An important feature was the discharge of the exhaust steam into the chimney to draw up the fire. Trevithick's locomotive successfully hauled 10 tons of iron ore and seventy passengers in five wagons at 5 miles per hour along a 10 mile line.

The following year a locomotive was built at Newcastle to Trevithick's design, for use on the Wylam wagon-way, and in 1808 he exhibited another locomotive, this time in London, which ran on a circular track laid on waste land near Euston Square. The public were offered rides in an open carriage behind the engine, at a shilling a head. This locomotive, called *Catch Me Who Can*, weighed 8 tons and ran at 12 miles per hour. But although Trevithick had succeeded in producing steam locomotives which were mechanically quite successful, the track upon which they ran was not strong enough to bear their weight and he was to become discouraged from further locomotive development. Some people thought that steam locomotives working by adhesion only would fail, because the smooth wheel would slip too much upon the smooth rail, and an attempt to overcome the problems of insufficiently strong rails and also to improve adhesion, was made by John Blenkinsop in 1811 using a cogged, driving wheel, which engaged a rack rail with

1 Stephenson's *Planet* type locomotive on the Liverpool and Manchester Railway, 1830. This engraving by Shaw shows the locomotive passing Rainhill Bridge.

teeth cast on one side. This method was employed on the Middleton colliery railway, Leeds, (which was first opened in 1758) and three locomotives were constructed by Mathew Murray during 1812-3, each with two double-acting cylinders driving two shafts, with cranks set at right angles. These crankshafts were both geared to a shaft carrying the large cogweel, which engaged with the rack rail. These three locomotives ran until 1835, and the rack-rail principle is still in use today on certain steep-grade mountain railways, including the Mount Washington line, USA.

The straight adhesion locomotive was, however, not destined to be abandoned and in 1813 William Hedley and Christopher Blackett designed a locomotive for the Wylam Colliery, where the original wooden rails had been replaced by cast-iron plates to allow the introduction of steam haulage.

This was the famous *Puffing Billy*. Both this and George Stephenson's first locomotive *My Lord* (later renamed *Blücher*), which was first steamed on the Killingworth Colliery tramway, on 25 July 1814, still suffered from the inadequate track. They had no springing, and derailments were numerous, because the cast-iron, flanged-plate rails were too fragile for their unsprung weight and ponderous movements. The future of steam locomotion seemed dim indeed, but Stephenson came across the fact that a new process for making wrought iron rails had been developed and patented in 1820 by John Birkinshaw, of Bedlington, Northumberland, and the success of this process enabled locomotive development to continue. Before this, Stephenson had built several 'steam-sprung' engines for low speed, colliery haulage, where the axles were free to move up and down in guides and were attached to pistons fixed to the underside of the boiler. The idea was that the pressure of the boiler steam maintained the wheels in contact with the rails, despite the inequalities of the track.

In 1825, only eighteen locomotives were doing useful work in England, out of a total of thirty built at various times, and no-one except George Stephenson had continued to build steam locomotives after 1814. Public opinion of the steam locomotives was not encouraging; the inevitable title of 'iron horse' was bestowed upon these strong but clumsy machines which threatened to replace the faithful horse, they were noisy and somewhat terrifying; they belched forth smoke, steam and red hot coals – was this brute creation really desirable?

The first public railway in the world, the Stockton and

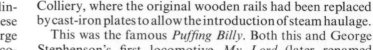

2

3 Darlington, was authorized in 1821 and George Stephenson was appointed engineer in the following year. One condition he made before accepting the post, was that he was to ensure that the tracks would be made strong enough to convey steam locomotives, although the Act of Parliament stated that the company was to work its traffic by 'men, horses or otherwise'. Stephenson read 'otherwise' to mean steam locomotion and gave the task of developing a suitable design to his son, Robert, and his associates at the firm of Robert Stephenson & Co., Forth Street Works, Newcastle. They produced the first engine, *Locomotion*, in time to run on the opening day, 27 September 1825, when she hauled twenty-two wagons containing between 400 and 600 passengers at a speed of 8 miles per hour.

During 1825 and the next few years, many new types of locomotive were tested upon the Stockton and Darlington line, and a particularly noteworthy improvement upon the original Stephenson engines was *Royal George* produced by Timothy Hackworth in 1827. This had six wheels and an arrangement of compensated levers to effect some degree of springing.

George Stephenson had by now turned his attentions to the problems of civil engineering and new railway construction, leaving his son to do most of the development in steam locomotive design. In 1828 Robert produced *Lancashire Witch*. This had four-coupled wheels driven by two inclined cylinders. The drive from the cylinders was taken by crankpins on the front wheels and both axles were sprung. Put to

2 Stephenson's *Rocket*, which was built at Newcastle-on-Tyne in 1829 to compete for a prize of £500 offered by the Liverpool and Manchester Railway Co. for the best locomotive. Five locomotives entered and 'Rocket' won.

3 The *Derwent* locomotive running on the Stockton and Darlington Railway in 1845.

4 The Hetton Colliery Locomotive, which was built by George Stephenson and Nicholas Wood. It was rebuilt in 1857 and again in 1882, when the present Link Motion was fitted.
4

5

5 A model of a locomotive designed in 1843 by the American engineer William Norris, a Philadelphian, which has a special four-wheeled swivelling bogie for use on lines having steep inclines and sharp curves. Austrian railways acquired one of Norris's locomotives and named it 'Austria'.

6 Contemporary model of the broad gauge locomotive 'Ixion', which was designed by Daniel Gooch and built for the GWR in October 1841. It was largely based on the design of *North Star* built by Robert Stephenson and Co. in 1837.

7 *Puffing Billy*, which was built at Wylam Colliery by William Hedley and Christopher Blackett in 1813, was used over a five mile stretch of track between Wylam and the staithes at Lemington-on-Tyne for nearly fifty years.

6

work on the Bolton and Leigh Railway, it weighed 7 tons and was capable of hauling a load of 50 tons up a gradient of 1 in 440 at a speed of 8 miles per hour. The old-style boiler was still perpetuated, but with two flues with a firegrate in each, exhausting through a single chimney.

By 1829 the design of steam locomotives had made little real progress and their future was still far from certain. When the construction of the Liverpool and Manchester Railway was authorized, the directors were uncertain whether to use locomotives, or stationary engines installed at the lineside to haul the trains by means of ropes. A committee was set up to investigate and report upon existing railways using both systems of haulage, and duly reported back in favour of stationary engines and ropes. Nevertheless, some of the directors, backed by George Stephenson's advice, continued to favour locomotives. Accordingly, the railway company offered a prize for a steam locomotive of improved design, which would successfully fulfil certain very strict conditions. In addition to the £500 prize money there would be purchase of the locomotive and a contract for more.

The important conditions, which the locomotives had to fulfil, included, that they should consume their own smoke and haul continuously a load equal to three times their own weight at an average speed of not less than 10 miles an hour. The trials were held between 8 October and 14 October 1829, on a level stretch of line at Rainhill, 9 miles from Liverpool. The locomotives entered for the trials were *Rocket* by Stephenson; *Novelty* by John Braithwaite and John Ericsson; *Sans Pareil* by Timothy Hackworth, and *Perseverance* by Timothy Burstall. In addition, a carriage propelled by means of a horse on a treadmill was entered by T.S. Brandreth, known as *Cycloped*.

The *Rocket* ran at Rainhill on 8 October 1829, hauling 12¾ tons at an average speed of 13.8 miles an hour; attaining a maximum speed of over 24 miles an hour on one trip. However, when running without a load, the *Rocket*, which weighed 4¼ tons, achieved a speed of 29 miles an hour. It was the only locomotive to fulfil the conditions of the competi-

tion and was awarded the prize of £500, and the locomotive contract for the Liverpool and Manchester Railway went to Stephenson's. *Rocket* had a multi-tubular boiler and in basic conception was to set the pattern for locomotive design and construction over the following 100 or more years. The use of fire tubes to convey the heat of the furnace from the boiler firebox through the water to a smokebox became standard locomotive practice.

Following the success of *Rocket*, public opinion swayed more in favour of the steam locomotive and the ensuing ten years saw rapid advances in the size, design and construction of engines, as a result of the demands of the Liverpool and Manchester Railway.

But before proceeding to describe these larger locomotives, mention should be made of the work of Marc Seguin, who was responsible for the first engine to be built in France, in 1829. He had patented a multi-tubular boiler in 1827 and one was fitted to his first engine. Perhaps the most unusual feature, and certainly the least successful, was the provision of two rotary fans, driven by the wheels, to provide a draught for the fire. It ran on the St. Etienne-Lyons Railway.

In England a number of locomotives similar to the *Rocket* but larger and heavier, and known as the *Northumbrian* type, were constructed between 1830-40; these were more than twice the weight of the *Rocket*. Also introduced in 1830 were the *Planet* type of locomotives, which had the cylinders placed inside the smokebox and worked direct onto a double-cranked, driving axle. For passenger working the four-wheeled arrangement was a 2–2–0, with small, front carrying wheel and large, rear driving wheel, but for goods haulage the four wheels were coupled. A similar design of goods engine was produced by Edward Bury in 1831. The *Liverpool* had two cylinders under the smokebox and four coupled 6 ft. wheels. The firebox had a high-domed crown of D section, instead of being rectangular as was usual practice at that time. The driver's platform was attached to the back of the firebox. Bury had been too late with his design to participate in the Rainhill trials, but some of his engines which were

8

STEPHENSON'S PATENT LOCOMOTIVE ENGINE.

exported to America, introduced the bar frame, which was to become a familiar characteristic of American steam design for the following century.

A problem common to all the four-coupled engines of the 1830s was the severe oscillation or 'pitching' which was experienced when the engine was travelling at even modest speed, due to the short wheelbase. This factor, plus a desire for larger engines to handle heavier loads as business flourished on the new railways, led Stephenson to the design of a six-wheeled engine, the *Patentee* type, which had a large, single, central driving wheel, with small carrying wheels at either end. The *Patentee* of 1834 was the basic prototype of the British single-wheeler passenger engine, which was to flourish for the next sixty years. *Patentee* locomotives were exported to several pioneer railways in continental Europe, including the Ludwigsbahn from Nüremberg to Fürth, which was opened by the Stephenson locomotive *Adler*. By 1835, just six years after the Rainhill trials the improved 2–2–2 passenger locomotives had cylinders of 12 in. or 13 in. diameter by 18 in. stroke, with driving wheels of 5 ft. or more in diameter. With a boiler having about 400 sq. ft. of heating surface and a grate area of 10 sq. ft. and a working pressure of 50 pounds per square inch, these engines were able to

9

work a load of about 50 tons at an average speed of between 20 and 25 miles an hour.

Although many strange inventions were to be matched against the Stephenson conception from time to time, other locomotive builders were quietly following his example. Locomotive development proceeded apace, matched by a virtual bonanza of railway construction and speculation; orders for new locomotives flowed in, and engineers were ac-

8 Stephenson's *Patentee* design, which incorporated an inside-cylinder 2–2–2 and was first produced in 1838. This shows a later example of 1843. It was a design which had a wide influence upon locomotive builders for more than twenty years.

9 Built in the late 1830s this 'Lion' locomotive is seen in an exhibition staged 100 years later to commemorate the centenary of the London and Birmingham Railway, 1938.

cordingly encouraged to pursue further improvements in the design and construction of their engines. One man who resolutely pursued a lone course in locomotive design was Edward Bury. He continued to introduce his small, bar-framed design (albeit improved by the addition of a rear carrying axle under the footplate) for service on the London and Birmingham Railway until 1846; by which time they were hopelessly outclassed and undersized.

In 1840 the Birmingham & Gloucester Railway imported some American-built locomotives, designed by William Norris of Philadelphia. Norris had already supplied the first locomotive for Austria, the *Philadelphia*, which was received in Vienna in April 1838, and others followed, so that by the end of 1843 at least ten Norris engines had been ordered from America. In 1844 the Americans, William and Octavius Norris left to set up a locomotive workshop in Vienna, but meanwhile their designs had been imitated by local locomo-

tive builders, and they were to receive few orders indeed. The first steam locomotive to run in Switzerland, *Limmat*, was of basically Norris design as built in modified form by Kessler-Karlsruhe.

A notable engineering advance in the 1840s was the use of steam expansively in the cylinders, by means of variation in the position of the valve gear. This 'link-motion' valve gear made use of two eccentrics on the driving-axle, one for forward and one for reverse running. The eccentric rods were attached, one at each end, to a curved 'link' containing a slot, in which a die-block attached to the slide valve of the steam chest, could slide. By moving the link, and so altering

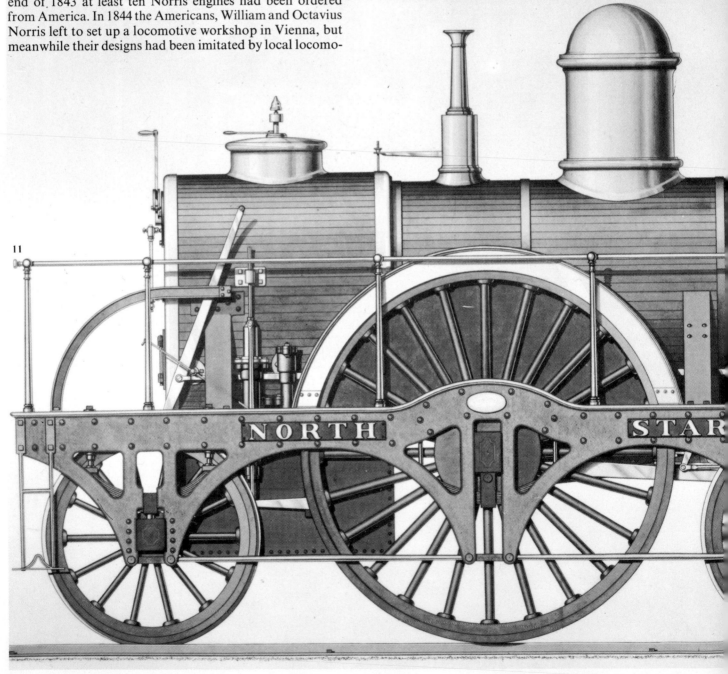

the position of the die-block, the direction of locomotive movement was determined. A partial movement of the die-block towards the centre of the link 'cut off' some supply of steam to the cylinder, before the piston had completed its stroke, thereby economizing fuel by using the steam expansively. Pioneers of link-motion were Alexander Allan, Sir Daniel Gooch and Robert Stephenson & Company, all producing reliable designs which remained in use for some sixty or so years, when radial valve gears, such as that of E. Walschaerts of the Belgian State Railways (who in fact introduced it as early as 1844), became modern practice.

Reverting to the late 1830s, attention in England had switched from the industrial North, where Stephenson and others had blazed the railway trail, to the lush pastureland of the West, where Brunel's Great Western Railway main line from London to Bristol was being planned on a scale, which in conception and construction, was without rival in the world. Brunel was a man of vision and wanted his railway to run on a larger gauge than the 4 ft. 8½ in. of Stephenson and followers. His lines were laid to a gauge of 7 ft. and for the opening in 1838 Brunel ordered twenty locomotives from various builders. They were unfortunately to prove an extraordinary collection of 'freaks', and only two, built by Stephenson, proved successful. These were *North Star* and *Morning Star*. Basically of *Patentee* type, they were originally built to the 6 ft. gauge for a line in the southern states of North America, but they were not shipped, due to financial problems, and Stephenson converted them to 7 ft. gauge for the Great Western. *North Star*, running between London and Maidenhead in 1838, hauled a load of 80 tons at a speed of over 30 miles an hour.

So successful were these two engines that Brunel's assistant Daniel Gooch, faced with the problem of building a stud of reliable new engines for the line, took Stephenson's design as the basis for his own *Firefly* class 2–2–2s, of which sixty-two were built to a standard specification by various firms between 1840-2. At the time, these locomotives were without equal in terms of power and speed.

In 1841 Stephenson patented a long-boilered locomotive with a barrel about 11 ft. 3 in. in length, as compared to the average at that time of about 8 ft. 6 in., with the additional length being provided to make better use of the fire tubes as heating surfaces. He also wanted to obtain a lower centre of gravity. Large numbers of 'long-boiler' engines were built up to about 1847 and proved particularly successful on the continent of Europe, but the British examples were not so happy, due to the fact that they had to retain a short wheelbase in order to fit the turntables then in use. This meant that all the wheels had to be crammed into the space between the back of the smokebox and the front of the firebox, with a considerable overhang at each end. Except for freight duties, where speeds were moderate, this wheelbase produced unsteady riding on British track.

10 The opening of the Stockton and Darlington Railway, 1825, by Terence Cuneo.

11 The 2–2–2 locomotive *North Star* supplied by Robert Stephenson and Co. to the broad gauge Great Western Railway, 1837.

17

Another attempt to reduce the centre of gravity, one which also proved to be more lastingly acceptable on the Continent, was conceived by Thomas Russell Crampton. His idea was to place a large, single driving wheel right back behind the boiler and firebox. The size of the driving wheels did not, therefore, limit the size of the fire-grate and he employed 7 ft. driving wheels for the first two 'Crampton' engines, which were built for the Namur and Liège Railway in Belgium in 1846. These engines were carried on six wheels; two carrying wheels spaced out under the boiler and the big driving wheel at the rear end with the enginemen placed on a footplate between two commodious splashers. They were fast runners with light express trains and in France and Germany they were very popular; nearly 300 were built for the Continent between 1846 and 1864, whilst in Britain a number of railways ran them up until 1875.

The largest 'Crampton' engine was built for the London and North Western Railway in 1848, and this engine had two cylinders of 18 in. diameter by 24 in. stroke and the driving wheels were 8 ft. in diameter. Used between London and Wolverton on heavy trains, the locomotive itself weighed 35 tons.

The theory that a low centre of gravity was desirable found its extreme expression in the design of *Cornwall*, by Francis Trevithick, built in 1847 for the London and North Western Railway. The boiler was placed below the driving axle, which had wheels of the exceptional diameter of 8 ft. 6 in. It was soon rebuilt to more conventional appearance. Even larger – 9 ft. – driving wheels were successfully used on the 4–2–4 express tank engines of the broad-gauge Bristol and Exeter Railway, built in 1853-4.

Whilst Stephenson, Crampton and Trevithick were involved in the developments just described, other locomotive builders were steadily producing their own, progressively improved versions of Stephenson's *Patentee*. Notable examples were the *Sharpies* of Sharp, Roberts & Company, built as their standard engine for many different railways, and perhaps most famous of all, the *Jenny Lind* design of David Joy for E.B. Wilson. By this time, locomotive appearance had progressed considerably, the crude manufacture of the early locomotives had given way to some beautifully refined

products with ornate finish and colourful liveries. The constant search for improvement was matched by greater sense of style. The *Jenny Lind* design was indeed a lovely machine to gaze upon, with nicely balanced proportions. (*Jenny Lind* was in fact the name of a great Swedish singer, who was at the time all the rage in England.) Speaking of the first of his *Jenny Linds* for the London, Brighton and South Coast Railway, Joy noted in a journal that the engine was 'finished regardless of cost. Boiler and firebox were lagged with polished mahogany and bound with bright brass hoops and brass finishings, the dome and safety valve tops were bright copper, and there was other bright work about that made her a very smart-looking engine.'

The evolution of the Stephenson *Patentee* through to such locomotives as the *Jenny Lind* had centred around the principle of an inside-cylinder 2–2–2 with double frames, and although some engineers continued to use double-frames for some time to come, it was realized by others that a pair of inside frames was quite adequate. Some favoured retention of inside cylinders, such as McConnell's *Bloomers* (to be discussed later) others, such as Ramsbottom on the Northern Division of the London and North Western Railway, favoured outside cylinders, as in his *Problem* class 2–2–2s.

By the year 1851, just over twenty years from the opening of the Liverpool and Manchester Railway, the steam locomotive had been transformed from a relatively unknown quantity, gamely trying to prove its worth, to an accepted machine with considerable influence upon everyday life. By this time locomotives were being constructed to increasingly large dimensions, with a view to obtaining greater power and improved performance. McConnell's *Bloomers*, already mentioned, broke away completely from the low centre of gravity theories of the 1840s and in many ways they were advanced machines for their day. The nickname *Bloomer* derived from the fact that they exposed a good deal of wheel below the running-plate at a time when a certain Mrs Amelia Bloomer was seeking reform in women's dress in England! The *Bloomer* class (there were extra large, large and small versions) had a bold, tall outline with a high running-plate, inside frames and bearings and inside cylinders.

13

12 *Jenny Lind*, the handsome 2–2–2 design by David Joy for E.B. Wilson, 1847.

13 The freakish 'Crampton' locomotive, which was ordered by Stevens and outshopped in 1849 for the Camden and Amboy line, USA, to English specification, and built by Isaac Dripps.

14 The interior of the Engine House, Swindon, with a Gooch 2–2–2 locomotive being placed upon the traverser. From a drawing by J.C. Bourne, 1846.

14

By this time the world had adopted the railway, as enthusiasm had spread across the Continent, and the European powers built railways in their overseas possessions. American engineers, forced to come to terms with the need for larger and more powerful engines capable of running over lightly-laid tracks, had conceived the idea of adding two, small, leading wheels, which acted as a pilot to the driving wheels. This was refined into the 'bogie', which had already been essayed in primitive form in England by Chapman and Hedley in pre-Stephenson days, but which was to lie dormant through several more decades of British locomotive development.

Locomotive design in the latter half of the nineteenth century was influenced by the need for greater speed, greater power and more economical working. Competition, and indeed open rivalries, forced railway managements to provide better services. Carriages got progressively larger and more comfortable, and of course heavier into the bargain. British engineers now accepted the bogie as a means of increasing the wheelbase of their locomotives without detriment to stability or flexibility. Brakes were improved; back in 1833 Robert Stephenson patented a steam brake, but it proved impossible to apply this to the trains as well as the locomotives, due to condensation problems, and manually operated brakes were used for carriages and wagons. Compressed air was used on American passenger trains by the late 1860s, and in 1875 George Westinghouse produced his air-brake design. But British engineers were of divided opinion about Westinghouse's invention, and an alternative vacuum brake was unfortunately persisted with for nearly ninety years on.

The outward appearance of British steam locomotives, by the year 1870, was of high artistic standard, whereas their Continental contemporaries were already beginning to display that love for external gadgetry which was to become their hallmark. Cross-fertilization of ideas between British, American and Continental locomotive builders was increasingly evident, but stylistic trends remained. The typical British locomotive of the last thirty years of the nineteenth century was a clean-faced affair with all the 'works' carefully

clothed or jacketed, and very graceful lines and curves. Such engineers as William Stroudley, Patrick Stirling, Samuel Waite Johnson and Dugald Drummond took considerable pains over the appearance of their locomotives, and their drivers were obliged to maintain them in absolutely spotless condition at all times.

The big, single-driver, passenger locomotive remained a favourite for express train working in Britain, but by 1880 the increasing size and weight of the trains was becoming an obvious embarrassment to their adhesion factor. Development of effective, steam-operated sanding gear (which placed sand on the rail surface immediately under the big driving wheel – thereby preventing wheel-slip) allowed a revival of the single-wheeler together with a leading bogie.

The decision to convert Brunel's broad gauge main line to the standard 4 ft. 8½ in., taken after much bitter argument and comparative trials, resulted in the need to restock the GWR with main line passenger engines. Daniel Gooch had followed his 2–2–2s (based, as mentioned earlier, upon Stephenson's *North Star*) with a class of eight-wheelers, the *Iron Dukes*, which, together with some virtually identical locomotives built by his successor William Dean, were responsible for the broad gauge main line trains to the end. But Dean also saw the possibilities of building some 'convertible' 2–2–2 engines, which would run on the 7 ft. until gauge conversion and could then be readily adapted to the 4 ft. 8½ in. They were 'ugly ducklings' indeed, until transformed (and later given a leading bogie to improve stability), when they became beautiful machines to gaze upon.

The search for greater efficiency in steam locomotion resulted in increased steam pressures and increased boiler capacity, relative to the capacity of the cylinders. Fuel economy was much desired, and compounding was one method which attracted many engineers. Marine engineering had successfully used the principle; one of turning the exhaust steam from one cylinder into another, to give an extra thrust. Anatole Mallet, a French engineer, applied the idea to a locomotive for the Bayonne-Biarritz Railway in 1872 and various systems were developed in Britain, America and on the Continent. Most successful were the applications by De Glehn and Du Bousquet in France, by Vauclain in America and Von Borries in Germany. The British contributions were not outstandingly successful, in particular the persistent efforts of Francis Webb for the London and North Western Railway. Despite some obvious deficiencies in the design, the autocratic Webb persisted with his compounds, and the far-off Pennsylvania Railroad purchased one, complete, of which little was subsequently heard. The Chicago World's Fair of 1894 had two Webb compounds on display. W.M. Smith on the North Eastern Railway produced a more reasonable compound engine and the Midland Railway subsequently built a successful class of compound 4–4–0s, which were perpetuated by the London Midland and Scottish Railway, after the 'grouping' of Britain's independent railway companies.

Another important development, which had a direct effect upon the efficiency and economy of steam working, was superheating. This involved the splitting-up of the steam on its way from the boiler to the cylinders, through a great number of small tubes placed inside the larger boiler flue tubes, so that the hot firebox gases dried the steam and

15 *Lady of the Lake* No. 531 of J. Ramsbottom's 'Problem' class single-drivers for the London and North Western Railway. Photographed outside Crewe works in May 1862.

16 The locomotive *Flying Dutchman*, a broad gauge express on the Great Western Railway in 1891. This photograph shows the mixed-gauge rails.

17 The 8 ft. single-driver by Patrick Stirling, which was built for the Great Northern Railway. No. 666 was built at Doncaster in 1881 (the design was introduced in 1870).

reheated it, before it passed to the cylinders, where it could therefore do better work. This principle was first successfully applied by Schmidt to two Prussian 4–4–0s in 1898, and only gradually won acceptance, but eventually it was to be so effective (when allied to piston valves and Walschaerts valve gear) that the added complication and expense of compounding was no longer justified; although French engineers were to persist with the principle right up until the final years of steam.

Locomotive development in America and on the continent of Europe had certainly overtaken Britain by the end of the nineteenth century, and most of the improvements came from these countries, although the basic locomotive concept of Stephenson was still adhered to. An influx of American-built locomotives was to be found on many Continental railways at this time, and in addition, some notable, indigenous locomotives had established fine reputations.

Back in the 1850s the Austrian Government had offered a prize for the best design for a locomotive to work the heavy gradients of their new Semmering line. Four contestants each failed to meet the conditions, but this event marked the beginnings of the articulated locomotive type, and one locomotive, the *Wiener Neustadt*, was the prototype of the Mallet type, which was eventually to include the largest and most powerful steam locomotives ever construc-

ted. Articulation found little British application, although the Beyer Garratt version was extensively exported to Commonwealth countries in the mid-twentieth century.

Tank engines were increasingly favoured in Britain during the latter part of the nineteenth century for short distance passenger trains. The tank locomotive carried its own fuel supply and did not require a separate tender. For goods trains the six-coupled, small wheeled locomotive became a great favourite and many hundreds were constructed by the various British railway companies, to designs which varied but little in basic principles. For passenger trains the 2–4–0 and 4–4–0 were beginning to oust the graceful single-drivers, as train loads became increasingly heavy and greater speed was required. It would be impossible to list in the space available all the beautiful, British, passenger locomotives produced at this time, but one or two should be singled out for brief mention. In particular, a series of fast passenger 0–4–2 locomotives designed by William Stroudley for the London, Brighton and South Coast Railway in 1876. These engines ran on the Brighton line for over fifty years. The period 1890-1900 saw the production of a whole series of classic 4–4–0 types. Those of Adams for the London and South Western Railway had the longest bogie wheelbase in the country, 7 ft. 6 in. and it gave them a very racy appearance. On the Continent also the 4–4–0 found increasing favour,

and on the Paris, Lyons and Mediterranean Railway the express type of the 1870s, a long boilered 2–4–2, was replaced in 1900 by a 4–4–0 design, whilst other French railways had introduced 4–4–0s of various types over the preceding eight years. Most British 4–4–0s had the two cylinders located inside, between the main frames, but increasing use was now being made elsewhere of the outside cylinder arrangement. One of the most famous 4–4–0 types for express duties was the *Dunalastair*, introduced on the Caledonian Railway by J.F. McIntosh in 1896, with enlarged versions following on in subsequent years. The Belgian State Railways closely copied this design for their express passenger work. Mention above of the new 4–4–0s for the Paris, Lyons and Mediterranean Railway is a reminder that these locomotives were notable for an early attempt at streamlining, in order to cut down wind resistance at speed. The design incorporated a prow-shaped smokebox door, and the chimney was pointed at the front, as was the front of the cab; these engines became known as the 'windcutters'.

Train speeds by 1884 had reached a maximum of about 75 miles an hour, and the normal loads of the fastest expresses were not much above 150 tons. Increasing use of longer and heavier bogie carriages, with greater passenger comfort, indicated a need for still larger locomotives. In 1898 the first 4–4–2 *Atlantic* type locomotive to run in Britain was introduced by H.A. Ivatt on the Great Northern Railway, and the first 4–6–0 express passenger engines were built by Worsdell for the North Eastern Railway in 1899, although a goods engine version had appeared on the Highland Railway five years earlier. Goods engines were also designed to be more powerful, and the eight-coupled, goods locomotive was increasingly favoured both in Britain and over much of Europe. Between 1900-10 the 4–6–0 passenger

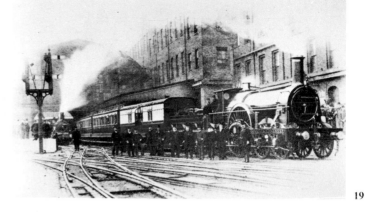

19

20

21

18 Broad gauge GWR locomotives at Swindon, following the conversion of the lines to standard gauge on 20 May 1892.

19 The last of the broad gauge locomotives to leave Paddington Station in 1892.

20 The Webb compound locomotive purchased from England by the Pennsylvania Railroad.

21 A long-boilered 2–4–2 express locomotive of the Paris, Lyons and Mediterranean Railway, constructed in 1881.

22 An East London suburban train of the 1870-80 period with the Stroudley 0–6–0T 'Terrier' design. No. 70 *Poplar*, at Selsdon Road.

22

23

24

25

locomotive and the 4–4–2 began to supersede the 4–4–0. Four-cylinder locomotives were developed, with driving wheels of 6 ft. to 6 ft. 9 in. diameter. On the continent of Europe compounding was still very much in favour, and the French engineers in particular had gained a considerable reputation for this development. In 1900 the Nord 4–4–0 compounds were capable of running the 95.1 miles from Paris to St Quentin, with the 'Nord Express' in 85¼ minutes, although the train weight was only 113 tons. In 1902 the first Nord, four-cylinder compound *Atlantics* were in service, and in the years 1903 and 1905, three, four-cylinder, French *Atlantics* were ordered by the Great Western Railway in England for trial purposes; of which more anon.

The limiting factors in new locomotive development in the opening years of the twentieth century were the rate that steam could be generated and the physical limitations of the loading gauge. Taking these in turn, the way to increase steam was to provide a larger firebox and grate, and development of the wide Wootten firebox in America, which overhung the main frames and required a small carrying wheel below, led to the wide-firebox *Atlantics*, and then to the even larger 4–6–2 *Pacifics*. The mighty *Pacific* was to be a favourite, express passenger locomotive in many parts of the world; on the Continent it made its debut in Germany and France before 1910 and in England the Great Western Railway introduced *The Great Bear* in 1908. Huge and heavy, it was, alas, ahead of its time in conception and remained the only *Pacific* to run in Britain for fourteen more years. The French experimented with even larger, express, passenger engines in 1910, when 4–6–4 *Baltics* were built by the Nord. These were exceptionally large for the period, with an overall length of 80 ft. 10½ in. over buffers and a weight of 100½ tons (156 tons with tender). Like *The Great Bear*, they proved to be ahead of their time, and it was the compound *Pacific* and 4–8–2 *Mountain* types which were to be developed by French railways for nearly a quarter of a century to follow.

The modern locomotive of 1910, whether British, American, French or German, still owed much to Stephenson and to an amalgam of progressive invention and cross-fertilization of ideas from one country to another. To Stephenson's basic, multi-tubular, boiler layout had been added the German invention of superheating and the Belgian Walschaerts valve gear and Belpaire firebox. Many American features were influencing designers in their quest for greater power, speed and efficiency. At Swindon, on the Great Western Railway, G.J. Churchward had taken office as locomotive engineer in 1902 and he introduced many changes to traditional British locomotive practice – certainly the style of a Churchward engine was completely new to British eyes; the principal features being the tapered boiler barrel with top feed (and no dome), the Belpaire, flat-topped firebox and medium-high running plate. He experimented with both the 4–4–2 and the 4–6–0 arrangement to determine what was best for the future and, as already mentioned, he purchased three French De Glehn compounds for comparison, before deciding upon the simple expansion 4–6–0 (both two- and four-cylinder versions). His designs represented the beginnings of the 'modern' school of British locomotive practice,

and were destined to have considerable influence upon the products of the next quarter century in Britain.

The other limiting factor in locomotive development, namely the loading gauge, was most serious in Britain, where engineers now had to pay the cost of being pioneers in the field of railways. The loading gauge was determined by the physical proportions of the various fixed installations and civil engineering works along the line. Thus, the width of bridges, the height of tunnels or the distance between cutting walls could limit the overall size of a locomotive or train. The need to respect clearances, which had basically been laid down when Stephenson was constructing Britain's first railways, was perhaps one reason for reflecting upon what might have been, had Brunel's 7 ft. gauge been adopted as a national – or international – standard, rather than the still restricted 4 ft. 8½ in. gauge. Certain countries, such as Spain, Russia and Ireland have more generous rail gauges (whilst America manages to carry far larger trains over the 4 ft. 8½ in.) but only Brunel's GWR main line was built with the optimism of a true visionary.

23 Special decorations placed on the London, Tilbury and Southend Railway 4–4–2T No. 61 *Kentish Town* on the occasion of the coronation of King Edward VII, 1902.

24 The Churchward four-cylinder 4–6–0 express passenger locomotive No. 4007 *Rising Star*, for the Great Western Railway.

25 A four-cylinder compound Pacific express passenger locomotive. Nord Railway of France.

26 No. 102 *La France*, a French-built compound Atlantic locomotive delivered to the Great Western Railway.

27 The solitary Pacific locomotive *The Great Bear*, introduced by the Great Western Railway in 1908.

2. ACROSS AMERICA

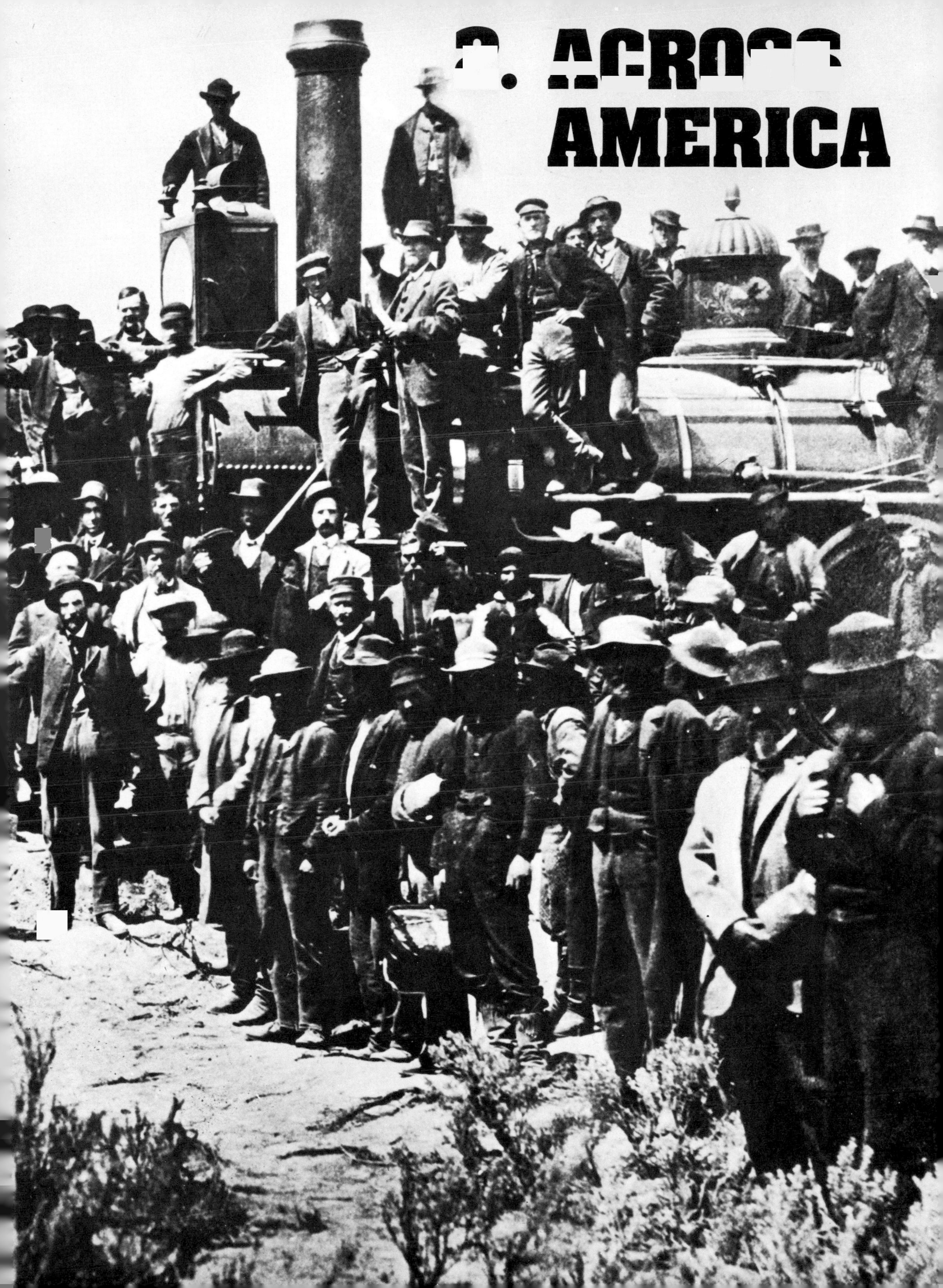

The European countries developed their railroads; the American railroads developed their country. This was the one fundamental difference between the railroads that came into existence in Great Britain and America in the 1820s and 1830s.

This point was clearly reflected in the development of the railway steam locomotive. The very first American locomotives, of course, were imported from Great Britain. But even such American-built locomotives of the 1830s as the *Tom Thumb*, *Best Friend of Charleston* and *De Witt Clinton* were counterparts of British locomotives. It was not long, however, before the US locomotive, shaped by the environment of the robust, new land, evolved along its own separate course. A swivel truck for non-powered front wheels was invented to help negotiate poor track. Pilots (or cow-catchers) were mounted on the frame at track level to protect the locomotives from obstacles on the tracks. When railroads began operating at night, headlights were placed on the boiler front to afford night vision – and provide a warning beacon – along the unfenced right-of-ways. The equalizer beam, which permitted each set of drive wheels to be independently sprung, was a major advance necessitated by poor track conditions. The drive wheels were counterbalanced to prevent hammer-like blows from being delivered through the wheels to the rails with each power stroke of the pistons and rods. Although most of America's technical innovations were eventually incorporated in locomotives found elsewhere in the world (just as developments from abroad were often incorporated in US engines), the American steam locomotive was never matched in the category of sheer physical size.

The forerunner of the large American locomotives was the 4–4–0 wheel arrangement introduced in 1836. This wheel arrangement became so widely used over the next four decades, that it was referred to as the American Standard, or the American type. The American type was in the vanguard of the rapid, railroad expansion from the Atlantic seaboard through the Ohio River Valley to the distant lands along the Mississippi River. American railroads cannot take credit for opening the land (wagons did that), nor for establishing commerce (canals and riverboats did that), but they were responsible for populating the land, and for providing the means of commerce to maintain that population.

Most early railroads did not come into existence as natural extensions of other railroads; instead they sprang up here and there to serve local interests. Railroad systems developed out of necessity, not out of grand design. Many railroads were undercapitalized and had to be built as inexpensively as possible. Others were built quickly – and poorly – to obtain land grants or franchises. With cost a critical factor, and with promoters thinking in terms of connecting towns together and not a country, it was only natural that a gauge was chosen that best fulfilled the limited aims set for the railroad. Thus early railroading displayed a great diversity in gauges – from 3 ft. to 4 ft. 8½ in. to 5 ft. to 6 ft.

But expand the railroads did. At the end of 1839, 2,818 miles of railroad track were in existence. Between 1840-50, 6,200 miles of additional railroad were built. For the years 1850-60, the construction figure increased to 21,600 miles. The stage was set for the decade of 1860-70, when railroading was to make its greatest impact yet on the young nation –

29

28 The meeting point of the Central Pacific and Union Pacific railroads at Promontory, Utah, 10 May 1869. Sam Montague (left) the Central Pacific chief engineer, with Jupiter behind, shakes hands with General Grenville Dodge (right), the Union Pacific chief engineer, with No. 119 behind.

29 An early American locomotive showing the cow-catcher on the front, take from a contemporary engraving.

30 The *De Witt Clinton*, the third locomotive to be built in the USA, hauling a train of passenger cars from Albany to Schenectady (New York), a distance of about 14 miles, on 9 August 1831.

31 The Locomotive Lion, which was brought to America by the Delaware & Hudson Canal Company from Stourbridge, England, where it was built, was the first locomotive to run in America at Honesdale, Pa., 8 August 1829.

W. & A. R. R.

first in a destructive vein, and then in a constructive vein.

The prelude to the destruction came on 16 October 1859, when an abolitionist named John Brown and a small band of his followers captured the federal arsenal at Harpers Ferry, West Virginia, as part of their militaristic protest against slavery. The dramatic raid highlighted the factionalism that was sweeping the country, between the slave holding states of the South and the free states of the North. The raiders were subdued when a detachment of United States Marines, under the command of Colonel Robert E. Lee (later to become the South's most famous general), rushed to Harpers Ferry over the Baltimore & Ohio Railroad.

Just as John Brown's raid foreshadowed the bloodshed of the Civil War, the railroad operation was a harbinger of the strategic and tactical roles railroads would play in the outcome of that war. Even before the Blue and Gray armies met in large-scale combat, the generals on both sides rushed troops into position to guard key, rail installations. During the first few months of the War between the States, the opposing armies merely skirmished, but on 21 July 1861, a large Feder-

al force under General Irvin McDowell engaged a Confederate army commanded by General Beauregard, in what was to become known as the First Battle of Bull Run. Indecisive fighting raged for hours, but by afternoon the Union troops appeared to be gaining the upper hand. Just then a fresh contingent of Rebel troops arrived to turn the tide and send McDowell's forces into retreat. The troops, under General Joseph E. Johnston, had slipped away from a Union force that was supposed to be engaging them in a side action, and had rolled to Beauregard's aid aboard trains of the Manassas Gap Railroad. For the first time in history, railroads directly determined the outcome of conflict between large armies.

Railroads went on to play a decisive role in the Civil War. Entire campaigns were planned around the logistical abilities of railroads. The quick and efficient movement of war materials from the industrial North to the war zones of the South

was dependent on the rails. Railheads and junctions became specific targets. Advancing armies moved to capture key, rail lines; retreating armies did all they could to destroy the railroads they left behind. Not only was the Civil War fought over and alongside the railroads, but many individual exploits of audacity and courage were directed against railroad targets. The Confederate cavalry general, Jeb Stuart, became a legend for his daring attacks far behind Union lines. The purpose of many of his attacks was to disrupt rail lines.

32. The *General,* the train which became world famous when James J. Andrews hi-jacked it to use against the Confederate army on 12 April 1862.

33

The most famous railroad adventure to come out of the Civil War involved the Andrews raid, that hi-jacked the locomotive *General*, which in turn has become the most famous 4–4–0 in the world. The story of this behind-the-lines action has been the subject of histories, novels and movies, and the locomotive itself – which was preserved and even restored to operation during the years 1962-6 – has been the subject of a recent custodial court fight between the state of Georgia and the city of Chattanooga, Tennessee (Georgia won in a US Supreme Court decision).

On 12 April 1862, a party of twenty Union soldiers in civilian disguise, led by a civilian spy, James J. Andrews, slipped into the small Southern town of Marietta, Georgia, and boarded a northbound train of the Western and Atlanta Railroad. Their mission was to capture the train and head north, burning bridges and destroying telegraph lines behind them, with the grand objective of isolating Chattanooga from the rest of the South and making it vulnerable to attack by a waiting Union army. During a breakfast stop at Big Shanty, eight miles north of Marietta, Andrews placed his men in one of three boxcars, uncoupled the passenger cars and boarded the locomotive cab, along with a Union engineer, who proceeded to speed the train out of town – all while the traincrew ate. With superb knowledge of railroad operations and schedules, and claiming he was carrying urgently needed gunpowder to the front, Andrews bluffed his way past two

stations, where his train had to meet opposing trains on the single track line. Meanwhile, William A. Fuller, the conductor of the train Andrews stole, took pursuit on a handcar. At a siding, he found an old steam locomotive, which he rode to the next station. The time it took Fuller to clear the track from obstacles and to exchange locomotives was offset by the time it took Andrews to place the obstacles and wait out meets with opposing trains. After enlisting the locomotive *Texas* in the chase, Fuller was able to quicken the pursuit. Thus, Andrews did not have time to burn the bridges, that were the object of the mission and that would have prevented further pursuit. The *General* ran out of steam, and Andrews and his men took to the woods, only to be captured shortly thereafter.

With the victory of the North in 1865 in history's first railroad war, the country turned to heal its wounds and establish new bonds. The most effective bonds were made of iron – iron that stretched from coast to coast in the form of twin rails. A railroad to California had been the dream of Americans as early as the 1840s. Between 1853-6 the Government made surveys of five, possible routes from the Missouri River to California, but Congressional partisanship for northern and southern routes resulted in a stalemate. The War ended that, of course, and a route was chosen that headed west from Omaha across the Nebraska and Wyoming territories. Working independently in the Far West, a young

civil engineer, named Thomas Judah, in 1860 surveyed a route east from Sacramento, California, through the rugged barrier of the Sierra Nevada mountains.

The Government did not build the railroad itself, but strongly subsidized private enterprise through the grants of bonds and lands. Two railroads came into existence: Judah helped to organize the Central Pacific (and then sold his interest) to build east from Sacramento; and Thomas Durant took control of the Union Pacific to build west from Omaha.

33 Building the Central Pacific railroad – the rock removed from the cut on the far hillside has been used to fill the slope.

34 A print showing a Central Pacific locomotive, complete with cow-catcher, carrying the United States mail across the Sierra Nevada in 1870. It also depicts the Chinese workers used to build the line.

35 A Union Pacific locomotive clearing the track of buffaloes in the early days of the railroad, 1871.

Construction began on both roads in 1863, but did not show signs of progress until the Civil War ended and resources and labour became plentiful. Although Civil War veterans and Irish immigrants pushed the Union Pacific 290 miles west in 1865 and 1866, Central Pacific (now directed by the Big Four of Charles Crocker, Collis P. Huntington, Leland Stanford, and Mark Hopkins) found its workers lured from the hard toil of railroad construction by the promise of easy wealth in the California gold fields. In desperation, CP put to work Chinese who had been houseboys and launderers. Their diligent work was so impressive, that the railroad imported thousands more from China, until Chinese performed most of the grading and much of the tracklaying of the Central Pacific railroad.

Across the American West, Union Pacific workers occasionally engaged Indians in fierce encounters, and at times troops had to guard the workers, but the overall Indian threat was minimal. A greater threat were the vices found in the 'hell on wheels' towns, that advanced west with the end of the track. Nature itself was the greatest obstacle, and the award of Government bonds and lands – waiting for the first of the onrushing railroads to claim them – was the greatest spur to progress. Central Pacific had to blast fifteen tunnels out of the granite walls of the Sierra Nevada, and cover 37 miles of track with wood snowsheds as protection against the ferocious snowfalls.

Word of the rapid progress across the land, that had been mislabelled the Great American Desert, astounded Europeans. One reason, no doubt, was that Europeans thought of railroads only in terms of the scientifically engineered,

massively constructed monuments of iron, stone and cement, that had joined so many of their cities in the previous three decades. America's Pacific Railroad for the most part used only the earth as ballast and used rough hewn timber for ties. The faster the lines were graded and the track went down, the faster the promoters could collect the mile-by-mile bonds. And if the cheaply laid line cost far less in expenses than what the bonds realized – well, that was just so much more money for the pockets of the promoters. Besides, there would be plenty of time to rebuild the lines later.

The race for bonds and lands became so absurd that at one point the CP and UP had surveyed and even graded hundreds of miles past the already completed track of the rival. Finally, it remained for Congress to choose the meeting point of the Central Pacific and Union Pacific. That meeting point was Promontory, Utah, where on 10 May 1869, officials from both railroads met to lay a golden spike in a laurel tie, drive a last spike to telegraphically signal completion of the 1,780-mile Pacific Railroad to the jubilant nation, and to watch as CP's locomotive *Jupiter* and UP's No. 119 symbolically touched pilots.

The *Jupiter* and No. 119 were as appropriate to the Promontory ceremony as a railway historian could ask. Naturally, they were 4–4–0s – the American Standards that dominated US railroading into the 1870s and 1880s. The *Jupiter*, designed for both freight and passenger service, was built by Schnectady in July 1868 and shipped around Cape Horn to California. She had drive wheels 60 in. in diameter and weighed about 65,400 pounds. Union Pacific No. 119, built by Rogers later in 1868, generally was similar to Jupiter.

37

The most readily apparent difference between the two loco-motives was the funnel-like, bonnet smokestack of *Jupiter*, and the tall, straight stack of No. 119. The bonnet stack contained a large, wire mesh, that trapped burning embers from the wood-fuelled fire of *Jupiter*, and the funnel design created space to retain the entrapped cinders. The smokebox, or the forward section of the boiler, on No. 119 was longer than normal, providing space for embers to burn out, before

36 An early American locomotive of 1875. Of typical American design it has outside cylinders and four coupled driving wheels, and a four-wheeled leading bogie out front. The bar type framing is almost universally adopted in America.

37 A train crossing the Niagara Suspension Bridge in 1859.

38 A contemporary print showing a train running along Broad Street, Philadelphia in 1876.

39 A Central Pacific locomotive on a siding near Salt Lake City, Utah, 1869.

they were either exhausted through the stack or collected at the bottom of the smokebox. Thus the straight stack was sufficient for the purpose of exhausting smoke. Both locomotives were capable of pulling a train of about 250 tons, which translated into fifteen to twenty freight cars at speeds averaging 10 miles per hour or five or six passenger cars at speeds of 25 to 35 miles per hour.

Brightly painted, decorated with gilt lettering and displaying highly polished brass and iron parts, *Jupiter* and No. 119 were the best of an exuberant era. The exuberance found expression in railway locomotives beginning about 1850, when gay colours and ornamental fittings provided a startling contrast to the more sombre appearance of the first steam locomotives. The locomotive was the foremost expression of man's genius, and it deserved the ornamentation of the same. The Civil War undoubtedly cast a cloud over such colourful excesses and this, coupled with the more practical demands of an industrialized America, led to the decline of ornamentation. The gay colours were just about history in the 1890s.

Hallmark that it was, the Pacific Railroad was only a spur to a railroad building boom across the West. A gauge of 4 ft. 8½ in. had been dictated by Congress for the Union Pacific and Central Pacific, thereby establishing a 'standard' gauge, that almost all new railroads of necessity would have to adopt. In 1870 the Northern Pacific laid its first track. Construction to the Pacific Northwest was interrupted by financial recession between 1873-9, but the railroad was finally completed in 1883. In 1870 Jim Hill took over the moribund St. Paul & Pacific Railroad and soon reorganized it as the Great Northern, and pushed the tracks west to Seattle, where they arrived in 1893.

South of the Union Pacific, Cyrus K. Holliday saw the first tracks of his Atchison, Topeka & Santa Fe pounded into place in the same year that the Pacific Railroad was finished. In succeeding years, the Chicago-California Santa Fe system was created. En route west, Santa Fe blocked the trackage and aspirations of William Jackson Palmer's Denver & Rio Grande Western, chartered by Denver citizens in 1870 ultimately to provide a rail link to Mexico. The D & RGW did turn west to reach Ogden, Utah in 1882, but its transcontinental ambitions were diverted by the discovery of silver and gold in the Colorado Rockies. Palmer had offered the exception to the new rule of building to standard gauge by constructing the D & RGW to a 3 ft. gauge, for the narrow gauge proved ideal for extending a vast system of tracks through the many mountain passes to tap the mineral wealth.

During these years of construction, the Big Four of the Central Pacific were not idle. Organizing new roads under the name of Southern Pacific, they expanded their hold on California and pushed the SP inland through the Southwest to New Orleans.

The transcontinental (actually a misnomer, because there are no true East Coast-to-West Coast, transcontinental railroads in the US) railroads helped to open the West, but some of the most notable population and railroad expansion took place in America's Middle West, where farmers and immigrants by the thousands settled in the rich agricultural states. To move grain and livestock to market – usually to Chicago, the 'hog-butcher' city of the world – the so-called Granger

railroads, such as the Burlington, Milwaukee, Rock Island and Chicago & North Western laced the prairie states with main lines and branch lines.

Most of the Midwestern and Western railroads were aided by Federal grants of lands. By making land grants of alternate sections of land on either side of the right of way, the Government sought to encourage railroad construction, and hence settlement, in sparsely populated territories. The provisions of the land grants are misunderstood by most Americans to this day. First of all, the lands were not given away, but the railroads had to agree to carry Government property and military personnel and equipment at one-half the established rates. This the railroads did into the 1940s, when they were estimated to have paid back – in reduced rates – over ten times the value of the lands at the time they were granted to the railroads. In addition, much of the land granted to the railroads was immediately sold to farmers, at the low prevailing rates, to raise money for equipment and construction. This, of course, was the exact purpose of the grants, and railroads generally did not retain the vast amounts of land to profit greatly from the subsequent hundred-fold increase in property values. (Exceptions would be the Northern Pacific and Union Pacific, which have benefited in recent years from mineral deposits found underneath otherwise barren lands.) Finally, of all the railway mileage in the United States, only about eight per cent was involved in the land grants.

The era of railroad building, and the railroad consolidation and acquisition that accompanied it, produced men of giant influence, who through legal and illegal manipulations dominated the financial life of America for almost half a century. The railroad moguls – or more unfavourably, 'robber barons' – operated in many ways. The owners of the Union Pacific and Central Pacific established their own construction companies, and then awarded contracts to these companies. Because these men did not have the patience or faith in the CP and UP as profit-makers, they sought a short-cut to wealth by paying excessive awards to their construction companies. This left the railroads with great debts and meant the stock of the promoters was worth little, but these men had already received millions of dollars in profit from their construction firms.

Not all of the drama took place in the West. Two kings of manipulators, Dan Drew and Cornelius Vanderbilt, fought each other through complicated stock transactions for control of the Erie and a number of eastern railroads, that Vanderbilt shrewdly built from smaller roads into the New York-Chicago, New York Central System. Both men profited, but at the expense of the Erie. Later, a lieutenant of Drew, Jay Gould, became president of the Erie and milked it far more. He was well on his way to earning his reputation as the most corrupt of all the railroad barons, when he went West and purchased a bankrupt Rio Grande. He then blackmailed Union Pacific into taking his Rio Grande shares at inflated volume through an implied threat to build west from Utah and engage in a rate war UP could ill afford.

Victimized by overcapitalized construction and such subsequent manipulations as Gould's, UP was bound to fail. Self-seeking tactics had left many railroads in a deplorable state, but in the late 1890s a man rolled onto the scene who was destined to put most of the pieces back together – so well, in fact, as to incur the wrath of a president of the US. Edward Harriman's performance in taking control of a small New York state railroad, putting it on its feet, and selling at a profit had led to a directorship on the Illinois Central. In 1890 he forecast the Panic of 1893 and had IC pursue a strong cash position to ride out the storm. UP faltered in 1893, and when its bonds came due in 1897 he used IC money to purchase the road. Then he poured enormous amounts of money into UP, making it a first-class property. With money he gained from mortgaging UP, he bought control of the giant Southern Pacific and instigated improvements. Harriman believed railroads should own stock in other roads to prevent ruinous rate wars, and his UP soon controlled B & O. But he died in 1909, and President Teddy Roosevelt's anti-trust action forced UP to divest its SP holdings. In the meanwhile, the Government established the Interstate Commerce Commission to help set rates and avoid rate wars, artificially high rates and discriminatory rates.

In the decade 1870-80, an average of 4,000 miles of track per year was built; from 1880-90 the figure jumped to 5,000 miles of track; the mileage dropped to an average of 3,000 in the years 1890-1900, reflecting the impact of the financial depression following the Panic of 1893; but construction soared to 5,700 miles per year between 1900-10.

But slowly and surely over these years, important, mechanical improvements were made. Passenger comfort was increased dramatically when George Pullman began building sleeping cars about 1867. Safety in train operation took a step forward in 1869, when George Westinghouse invented the air brake, and then made a milestone advance, when the industry accepted Westinghouse's improved air brake in 1887. (Before the adoption of the air brake, each car in the train had to be slowed manually by a brakeman turning a wheel linked to the car brakes.) Semi-automatic couplers, with 'knuckles' to grip firmly the coupler of the next car, replaced the dangerous link-and-pin method of joining cars together. The refrigerator car was developed, that held ice in one compartment and shipments in another, so that fresh fruits and vegetables and dressed meat could be transported long distances. Steel rail supplanted iron rail.

It was the advent of heavier, steel rail that permitted larger locomotives to be built. Initially, larger locomotives were developed by merely adding more drive wheels. The 4–4–0 was enlarged to the 4–6–0. For heavy freight service, the 4–6–0 was enlarged to the 4–8–0. The eight-drive-wheel arrangement, in fact, began its widespread popularity in freight hauling, when a Lehigh Valley master mechanic, Alexander Mitchell, designed the 2–8–0 in 1866. The 2–8–0 was actually an outgrowth of the 2–6–0 Mogul type, which had been introduced in 1850, but had not appeared with a swivel pony truck until 1860. The first successful Moguls were constructed in 1865 and turned in excellent performances in fast, heavy freight service. Although 2–6–0s were built in the US as late as the 1920s, they were almost immediately and thereafter forever overshadowed by the popular 2–8–0s. The advent of the 2–8–0 brought to an end – for sixty years at least – the era of the dual-service (freight and passenger) locomotive. Known as Consolidation types, the 2–8–0s made their first major inroads about 1875. They hauled 1,000-ton,

42

40 In 1959 the Reading Company began a series of fifty excursion runs in eastern Pennsylvania. Flags are flying on No. 2100 on a run from Philadelphia to West Milton.

41 Clearing a snow drift on the Union Pacific Railroad, 1870.

42 No. 15 seems to have run out of steam on its climb in the Sierra Nevada in the 1870s.

43

44

Pre-war colour photographs of two American locomotives.

43 A Mallet 2–8–8–0 locomotive No. 202 on the Utah Railway at Helper, Utah.

44 A Mallet 0–8–8–0 locomotive No. 107 of the Kennecott Copper Co. at Magna, Utah.

eighty-car freight trains at 14 miles per hour on the Pennsylvania Railroad, which adopted them as its standard freight locomotive. On the Erie, operating experience showed that fifty-five 2–8–0s could replace 100 4–4–0s in freight service. Orders poured in so fast, that during the 1880s the noble 4–4–0s were relegated mainly to passenger service. It is estimated that 33,000 Consolidations were built for US railroads, making it the most numerous of all locomotive types. The 2–8–0 survived to the end of the steam era, when it was still used in switching and branch line service.

Accompanying the transition to single-purpose locomotives was a transition in fuel. Wood was the dominant fuel in

early American railroading, because it was extremely plentiful, easy to burn, and left few ashes. The pioneer railroaders were not unaware of the potential superiority of coal. Coal was burned in many locomotives during the 1830s, but the coal then available was anthracite, or 'hard' coal. It was a difficult coal to keep fired in the small locomotive fireboxes, and it burned too slowly to provide the rapid combustion required for production of steam. Only the Baltimore & Ohio, which tapped fields of bituminous, or 'soft' coal, used coal in the majority of its locomotives. The greater heating properties of coal were finally utilized, once general industrial demand resulted in the opening of more bituminous mines.

Many railroads across the country served these mines and the cost of mined coal was consequently reduced. After the Civil War coal was accepted as the best fuel, and by 1880 only ten per cent of the fuel burned was wood.

Even anthracite was primed for a comeback. An unusual style of locomotive, called the Camelback or 'Mother Hubbard', flourished in the East in the late nineteenth century, when the railroads serving the anthracite fields of eastern Pennsylvania and southern New York determined to make use of the native fuel. John Wootten, general manager of the Philadelphia & Reading, designed a firebox so wide, that it could successfully burn anthracite waste coal. Also, because

45 Union Pacific's *General Sherman*, which was brought to Omaha by steamboat from St. Louis on 8 June 1865.

46 The *General Haupt* locomotive, which was used during the American Civil War.

47 The *Queen Empress*, built in 1893 and sent to the Chicago Exhibition where it gained the gold medal. It is specially painted white with the Royal Arms in honour of Queen Victoria's Diamond Jubilee, 1897.

48 The *Josephine*, a Denver & Rio Grande Fairlie type locomotive with cow-catcher at each end, 1873.

49

49 A Mikado 2–8–2 in New Orleans, Louisiana.

50 A Consolidation type 2–8–0 locomotive in New Orleans, Louisiana.

51 A Mogul 2–6–0 locomotive at Blanca, Colorado.

50

the firebox was so wide, it had to be placed above – and not inside – the rear drive wheels. Since it already was as wide as track clearances would permit, there was no room to place the engineer in the customary position alongside and behind the firebox. Wootten moved the cab ahead of the firebox, so that it straddled the boiler midway in the length of the locomotive. The engineer was actually separated from the fireman, who had a small platform at the rear of the locomotive from which to shovel coal into the firebox. Camelbacks operated from 1887 until the early 1950s, although further construction was banned by law in the early 1900s, when rod failures injured crewmen riding in the dangerous position above the drive wheels.

Progressively larger boilers demanded more heating surface in locomotives that burned soft coal, too, and the answer in this instance was to make the firebox longer and deeper. To support the added length, two smaller wheels were placed behind the drive wheels. Thus, the so-called trailing truck permitted a large firebox with increased combustion ability at no increased weight on the drive wheels. Progress created more problems. Fireboxes became so large, that they strained the physical strength of the firemen who had to shovel coal into them. The mechanical stoker solved this problem. Although mechanical stokers became commonplace on American locomotives, they were comparatively rare elsewhere in the world, being used only on the largest locomotives.

The advent of the trailing truck led to the appearance of new wheel arrangements. In 1897 an American manufac-

turer delivered 2–8–2 locomotives to the State Railways of Japan, and the Mikado type was born. Affectionately known as Mikes, these locomotives were purchased by American railroads in their thousands, and if one had to choose a single locomotive that most symbolized the steam engine in America, it would probably be a Mikado type.

Passenger train motive power was not neglected. Although a 'modern' 4–4–0 numbered 999 had set a world speed record of 112.5 miles per hour over the New York Central & Hudson River in 1893, most passenger trains required the extra pulling power that only a larger engine could provide. The 4–6–0 and 4–4–2 were already part of the answer, but it was not until 1901 that Baldwin Locomotive Works built the first 4–6–2 Pacific type for New Zealand. Overnight the design caught on at home and for the next thirty years Pacifics dominated American passenger schedules as much as Mikados dominated freight operations. As popular as the Pacific type was, it lacked the weight and number of drive wheels needed to haul long trains over the many mountain areas of America. In 1912 an additional pair of drive wheels was added to the design, and the 4–8–2 or Mountain type came into existence.

The power of steam locomotives made a major advance when a method was perfected to reheat or 'supersaturate' the steam. During the nineteenth century, the steam produced in the boiler was simply piped into the cylinders, where it pushed the pistons back and forth. Early in the twentieth century, locomotive designers arranged the pipes in a circuit to pass back through the boiler, so that the steam was exposed a second time to the hot gases rushing from the firebox to the smokestack. The steam was heated to its saturation point, greatly increasing its expansion. Only then was it fed into the cylinders, where it expanded against the pistons with powerful force, giving steam locomotives (especially the two-cylinder, American locomotives) their distinctive 'barking', exhaust sound.

Through these progressive improvements, the art of steam locomotive design was ready for a quantum jump forward – an advance into an era of Super Power, that would produce the mightiest steam locomotives the world has ever seen.

52 The 2–6–0 Mogul type No. 6, which was built by Alco in 1909 for the East Jordan & Southern Railway.

What, in retrospect, may well be described as the most exciting phase in British steam locomotive development during the twentieth century, arose from the need for increased speed for express passenger services, which had become a matter of some urgency in the mid 1930s. Several factors contributed to this state of affairs, in particular, the ever-increasing, competitive threat of the internal combustion engine, both on the roads and in the air, and the fact that Britain was being left behind by the USA, Germany and France in the realm of rail speed. Whilst the preceding fifteen years had witnessed some excellent, individual, locomotive speed achievements, these were isolated cases, and the average speed of the British express passenger train had not progressed much since before World War I; remaining below, rather than above, 60 miles per hour.

Some splendid new, locomotive designs had emerged during the 1920s, including Gresley's Pacifics of class A1 (later improved as A3); Fowler's 'Royal Scots' for the LMSR; Maunsell's 'Lord Nelsons' for the Southern and the Collett 'Castle' and 'King' class 4–6–0s for the GWR. Each

of the 'Big Four' railway companies had built up a new and reliable stud of modern express engines since the 1923 amalgamation, and by 1934 locomotive design had advanced to the stage where the path to improvement lay in technical refinement, rather than in mere increased size. In fact, the rigorous British loading gauge was making its presence increasingly felt, and the limits in the overall dimensions for a high-powered, steam locomotive were becoming a real restriction to the designer. To take an example: the smokebox on the Fowler 'Royal Scot' 4–6–0 was so large in diameter that there was room only for a mere pimple of a chimney to be placed on top!

All these new locomotives represented the latest refinements in locomotive engineering which had developed from the trend first established in the nineteenth century – namely larger and more powerful locomotives to cope with the ever-increasing weight of trains. Elsewhere in the world, however, an alternative thesis was being developed, wherein the train load was strictly limited and operated at high speed, well within the haulage capacity of the locomotive.

Significantly, in Germany, France and America, diesel traction was being seriously developed alongside steam as an alternative mode of traction for high speed, passenger trains.

It was the success of one train in particular, the German, two-car, diesel-powered railcar 'Flying Hamburger' service, running between Berlin and Hamburg (178.1 miles in 138 minutes) that attracted the serious attention of the British locomotive engineer, Nigel (later Sir Nigel) Gresley. He suggested that a similar train could be purchased for trials on the LNER between London (King's Cross) and Newcastle. However, when approached, the German builders could not promise such attractively high speeds over the gradients and route restrictions of the British main line, and it also became apparent that the standard of comfort offered by a diesel set would be well below that already being given to British rail travellers.

53 A line-up of Collett 'King' class 4–6–0 locomotives of the Great Western Railway.

54 Experimental semi-streamlining applied to the GWR 'Castle' class 4–6–0 locomotive in 1935, in an attempt to reduce wind resistance; a similar experiment was applied to a 'King' class engine.

55 Maunsell's 'Lord Nelson' class 4–6–0 express passenger design for the Southern Railway.

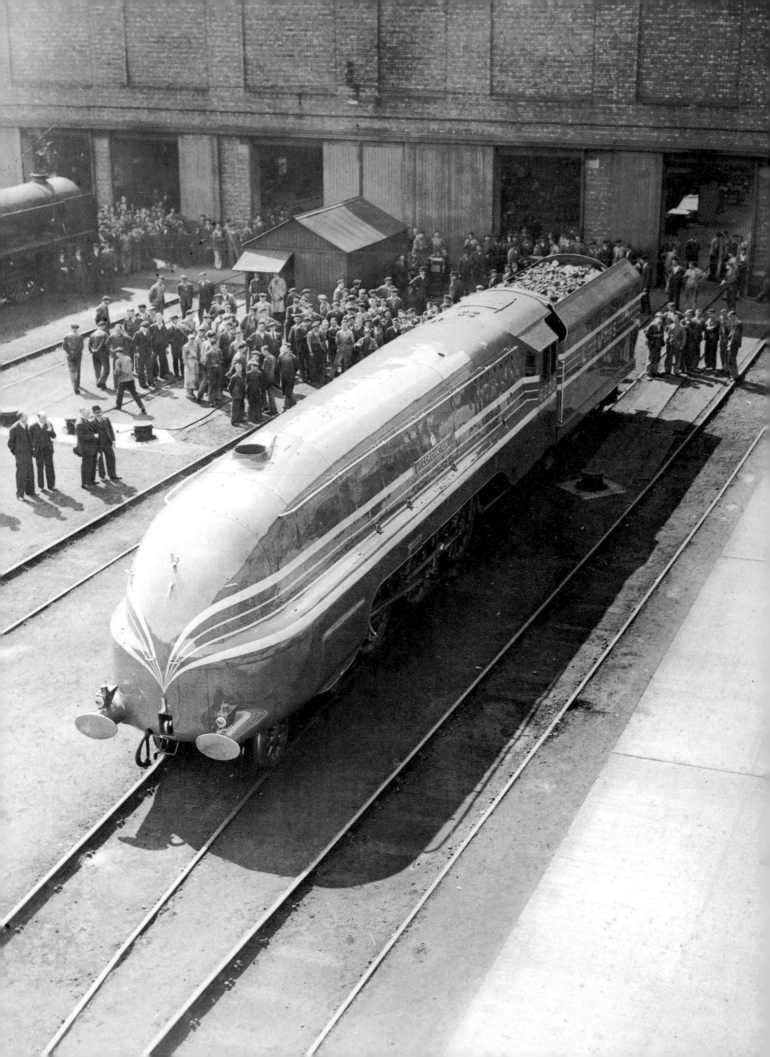

Gresley accordingly turned his attention to the feasibility of a lightweight, high speed train, with superior passenger comfort, to be hauled by a steam locomotive. The autumn of 1934 witnessed some preliminary trials between King's Cross and Leeds, 185.8 miles, with the standard Pacific No. 4472 *Flying Scotsman*, in which a load of 207 tons was hauled in the southbound direction in 157¼ minutes at an average speed of 70.8 and with a maximum of 100 miles an hour. The following March a test with a more recently built Pacific No. 2750 *Papyrus* was held between King's Cross and Newcastle and back, with six coaches weighing 217 tons. The round trip was made in one day and demonstrated most convincingly the feasibility of running regular, four-hour, steam hauled expresses of strictly limited load between the two cities, cutting no less than one hour from the existing best. During this trial *Papyrus* created four new world records for steam traction, which were: to run a distance of 12.3 miles at 100.6 mph; to run an aggregate 500 miles in one day at an average of 72.7 mph; to run an aggregate of 300 miles in one day at an average of 80 mph,

56 A view from above of the finished *Coronation*.

57 *Coronation*, first of the LMSR Stanier streamlined Pacifics, under construction at Crewe Works, 1937, showing the application of the streamlined steel casing underway.

58 The up 'Silver Jubilee' express passing Oakleigh Park at about 80 mph, hauled by an LNER class A4 streamlined Pacific locomotive No. 2512 *Silver Fox* designed by Sir Nigel Gresley.

and to achieve a maximum speed of 108 mph.

To make absolutely sure that a reliable new service could be introduced, it was decided to design a modified type of Pacific locomotive, which would be based upon the highly successful A1 and A3 class locomotives, whilst embracing certain important modifications to fit them for the high speed operations envisaged. Study of the performance of the existing LNER Pacific locomotives, showed that improvements could be made to boiler, firebox and cylinders, in order to obtain maximum efficiency, when running at high speeds. External streamlining was already an acknowledged means of reducing air resistance at high speeds. Although research into this factor was still in its infancy for rail application, it had been proved that reduction in the number of surfaces on the locomotive and train which encountered air resistance, could allow greater speeds to be attained for the same given horsepower. Thus streamlining seemed technically desirable. But there was also the undoubted publicity value which streamlining the new train would create; it was a fashionable mode for the time, and one which the railways could well benefit from, if they were to convince the public that they were not being left behind, in terms of progress, by the motor-car and the aeroplane. Thus the decision was taken that the new Pacifics would be fully streamlined externally, and the complete train would receive similar treatment.

Four, streamlined locomotives known as class A4 were ordered to be built for the initial service, of which the first to appear was No. 2509 *Silver Link*. The streamlining was applied with great care, following extensive experimental research at the National Physical Laboratory. The front end of the locomotive resembled a gigantic wedge, cutting through the air and causing a strong up-current of displaced air when the engine was in motion. *Silver Link* and her three sisters were finished in a special colour scheme of three shades of grey and aluminium, and the seven carriages had a similar treatment. This was the year of the Silver Jubilee of King George V's reign, and the complete train was accordingly named the 'Silver Jubilee'. On 30 September 1935 the first regular service of the new ultra-high-speed train was introduced, but the ability of the new locomotive and train was convincingly demonstrated three days earlier, when a special trial trip was made. Several world railway records

were broken on this occasion, with a maximum speed of 112 miles per hour twice being reached.

To celebrate the coronation of King George VI in 1937, the LNER planned another, somewhat heavier, high speed train, aptly named the 'Coronation', to run between London (King's Cross) and Edinburgh in just six hours. Five, further, streamlined A4 Pacifics were built, but the colour scheme was altered to two shades of blue for locomotive and train; the journey involved a considerable amount of high speed running. A similar train called the 'West Riding Limited' also made its appearance in 1937.

Naturally, the rival route to Scotland, operated by the LMSR was quick to react to the LNER achievements, and the result was that 1937 witnessed the introduction of another streamlined train named in celebration of coronation year. This was the 'Coronation Scot' and the booked time between London (Euston) and Glasgow was 6½ hours over a much more arduous route. William (later Sir William) Stanier produced a new 'Pacific' design which was to prove one of the best express passenger types ever to run in Britain. This was the 'Princess Coronation' class, of which the first, No. 6220 *Coronation* emerged from the Crewe works in May 1937. Like the LNER Pacifics, a streamlined exterior (but of somewhat different aspect) was adopted, with a blue and silver colour scheme for locomotive and train. A special test run in June 1937, by No. 6220, witnessed a top speed of 114 miles per hour on Madeley Bank, near Crewe. The following year the LNER reclaimed the publicity speed laurels by achieving 126 miles per hour with the A4 Pacific locomotive *Mallard*; a world record for steam traction which remains unbroken.

These special, high speed trains on the Anglo-Scottish routes did a great deal to restore public interest in rail travel, and their spectacular appearance gained much favourable comment; whilst their high standard of comfort was deeply appreciated. The world speed record of *Mallard* and the daily exploits of the new, streamlined trains showed what technical progress had been made with steam traction in Britain. Elsewhere in the world, similar attention was being paid to the potential benefits of streamlining for steam locomotives designed to operate at continuous high speeds, and it seemed that the conventional, steam locomotive still offered a fruitful field for development. In Germany an

advanced design of streamlined, 4–6–4 express locomotive had been produced, intended for speeds of 105 to 110 miles an hour, and had been credited with a maximum speed of 119 miles an hour, whilst a smaller, streamlined, 4–6–4 tank locomotive had also been designed for short-distance, high-speed trains. The United States railroads had also introduced streamliners on a number of important routes (al-

59 The *King George V* standing in the station before setting off in 1927.

60 Front end of a streamlined Pacific locomotive used on the Nord Railway, France, 1936.

though the diesel was beginning to make significant progress as an alternative) and one of their fastest, steam-worked, streamline trains was the 'Hiawatha', hauled by a 4–4–2 design, which ran the 280.8 miles between Chicago and La Cross (Wis.) in four hours and eleven minutes, at an average speed of 67.1 miles per hour, including three stops, and covered the entire 410 miles to St Paul in 6½ hours. The New York Central railroad had a completely streamlined locomotive in 1935 known as the *Commodore Vanderbilt*, which was one of their famous 4–6–4 'Hudson' locomotives specially modified; it frequently worked on the *Twentieth Century Limited*. A modified version appeared the following year, 1936, known as the *Mercury*, and the same year witnessed the introduction of the Pennsylvania Railroad's streamlined engine, with streamlining designed by Raymond Loewy. More than 100 wind-tunnel tests were made before the final shape of this locomotive was decided, using small clay models. At maximum speeds a $33\frac{1}{3}\%$ reduction in air resistance was claimed because of streamlining.

To return to Britain; the LMSR 'Coronation Scot' train

61 The driver and fireman standing in the cab of the *Lord Nelson*, which at this time, 1935, was the Southern Railway's most powerful engine.

62 Raymond Loewy's streamlined Pacific locomotive No. 3768 (nearest camera) built for the Pennsylvania Railroad USA. The photograph also shows two other types of streamlined electric locomotives and an older steam locomotive of conventional appearance, 1936.

63 The Fowler 'Royal Scot' class 4–6–0 locomotive No. 6139 *Ajax* passing Bushey with the down 'Royal Scot' express, 1932/3.

of 1937 was to be replaced by a new train for the 1940 service, with carriages of more luxurious appointment. Further streamlined (and one batch of non-streamlined) Stanier Pacifics were constructed, but with the colour scheme altered to crimson and gold. Sufficient carriages for the new train were finished in time to be sent to the New York World's Fair of 1939, and one of the newer locomotives went with them. It was actually No. 6229 *Duchess of Hamilton*, specially renumbered as No. 6220 *Coronation* for the purpose. The train made quite an extensive tour of American railroads, before going on show, visiting Washington, Philadelphia, Pittsburg, Cincinnati, St Louis, Chicago, Detroit, Cleveland, Buffalo, Albany, Boston and finally New York. The Fair was scheduled to run until 1 October 1939 and the outbreak of war between Britain and Germany on 3 September 1939 left the 'Coronation Scot' train well and truly stranded! The engine was eventually shipped back to aid the war effort, but the carriages remained in the United States for the whole duration of World War II.

The outbreak of war signalled the abrupt end of the short-lived, but glamorous, British, streamlined steam era, which had represented the peak of a train service which was the finest ever offered with steam haulage. The prestige and publicity value had been tremendous, and the locomotive achievements absolutely first class. But under wartime conditions there was no call for high-speed running, and the practical value of streamlining was lost. In fact, the streamlined outer-casings of the LNER and LMSR Pacifics were of no functional value for wartime trainloads, and even proved to be a hindrance to sorely pressed maintenance

staff. In due course of time the useless deadweight of these casings was removed entirely from the LMSR Pacifics, whilst it was partially cut away on the LNER engines, and the gay colour schemes of their pre-war days gave way to sombre austerity black.

The high-speed streamline era was never to return to Britain's steam railways, and the final, steam locomotive designs had a strictly functional appearance, in keeping with the immediate, post-war, utilitarian way of life. But today we are witnessing a return to streamlining on rails, with the careful, aerodynamic forms created for the very latest diesel, gas-turbine and electric, high-speed passenger trains, such as those on the Japanese Tokaido line, the French 'Turbotrains' and the revolutionary new British Advanced Passenger Train (APT), where the need to cut air resistance is once again an important technical consideration.

65 In America, just as in Great Britain, fame and fortune accrued to the first men who harnessed the power of steam into workable locomotives. Names of such inventors as Peter Cooper, who built the *Tom Thumb*, John Jervis, who developed the pony, or 'bogie' truck, and William Norris, whose locomotive *George Washington* hauled a cargo up a steep grade, received historical recognition. In this vein Matthias Baldwin is remembered as a jeweller who left his trade in 1825 to help open a machine shop, that soon began building stationary steam engines, and then – in 1832 – constructed a steam locomotive, *Old Ironsides*. But speak of Baldwin today and the image comes to mind not of a young scientist-machinist but instead of the mammoth Philadelphia, Pennsylvania foundry and erecting hall that bore his name, an industrial giant that in the course of 117 years placed nearly 70,000 steam locomotives on railroads right around the world.

Such associations marked an important difference between the appreciation of steam locomotives in America and England. For in England the cult of the designer not only

remained, but gained such impetus, that the ultimate recognition of knighthood awaited the most proficient locomotive architects. Sir William Stanier, Sir Nigel Gresley, as well as G. J. Churchward and R. E. L. Maunsell, were names directly associated with sparkling jewels of high-speed, meticulously-engineered locomotives. The booming country of America needed not jewels; it needed locomotives – a peak number of 65,000 of them on mainline railroads in 1924, for example, and there simply was neither time nor opportunity for one man to stamp his imprint on a locomotive and become famous for it. A few tried, and even succeeded, but to this day American locomotives are known by their builders and the railroads that operated them, and not by their designers.

Shortly after the turn of the century, locomotive construction in America was big business, and a once, large number of small builders had either fallen by the trackside or were merged into the 'Big Three' of steam locomotion: Baldwin, American Locomotive (Alco), and Lima. Lima was the smallest and the upstart. Yet it remained for Lima to propel the steam locomotive into the twentieth century. In 1925, at a critical time in the history of railroad transportation, Lima produced its experimental locomotive, A-1. The economy was growing, but the railroads could not keep pace, and service was beginning to stagnate. In fast, freight operation the locomotives of the day were severely limited in the number of cars they could pull. Most freight was pulled by powerful, but ponderous 'drag' locomotives, that could haul long trains, but at a pace that required many days for shipments to travel several hundreds of miles. The shippers needed faster schedules and the railroads wanted more efficient locomotives.

Lima responded with A-1. For speed, the A-1 employed eight, 63 in. diameter drive wheels, equalling the largest size wheels commonly accepted for freight service at that time. But more important, to maintain that speed, the A-1 had a large boiler operating at the relatively high pressure of 240 pounds per square inch. To insure that the steam was generated most efficiently, the A-1 featured a device (already perfected in Europe) called a 'feedwater heater', which first preheated the water from the tender, instead of injec-

64 From left: the 'Diamond Stack' No. 35, in use from 1850 onwards; the Mikado type No. 4960, built in 1923 for freight service; the Burlington 'Zephyr' diesel locomotive, introduced in 1934; the General Motors E-19 passenger unit, used today on high-speed 'Zephyr' passenger trains; the General Motors turbocharged GP-35 for fast freight service built in December 1963.

65 The Reading Company's No. 2100 and 2102 on an excursion run at Port Clinton, Pennsylvania.

66 A Pacific 'K' 4–6–2 locomotive No. 3406 which ran on the New York Central in 1920.

ting it cold into the boiler. And to make sure that the large boiler would be exposed to the heat in order to make steam to capacity continuously, a huge firebox was placed behind the boiler. The firebox was so large, that it necessitated a four-wheel, trailing truck to support its weight. Thus a new wheel arrangement, the 2–8–4, was introduced to everyday American railroading. The A-1 barnstormed the country, proving that it could haul longer trains at much faster speeds than the older 2–8–0s and 2–8–2s. To make sure it lugged those long trains out of the yards and got them rolling to the high speed, where a steam locomotive reaches its peak power, the A-1 employed still another recent innovation: a booster loco-motive. The large trailing truck beneath the locomotive cab housed its own small engine. Steam from the locomotive boiler was fed through this engine, which turned a gear that could mesh with a gear built around the centre part of one of the trailing, truck axles. The extra turning power from the small wheels was ideal for delivering the traction necessary to move a heavy train from a standing start. The booster gears

were disengaged once the train was moving at a steady speed.

Lima called its new, high-horsepower locomotive 'Super Power', and when the first production versions were put to work by the Boston & Albany in New England's Berkshire mountains, the 2–8–4 received the nickname Berkshire. The 2–8–4 wheel arrangement was gradually refined into an even more efficient and high-speed locomotive. Most locomotive students agree that the finest Berkshires of all were used by the Nickel Plate Railroad on its main line from Buffalo, New York, to Chicago, Illinois, and St. Louis, Missouri. Because the Nickel Plate did not have many on-line industries to supply traffic, and because its main line closely parallelled (often within sight) the tracks of the great New York Central System, it was placed in a precarious competitive position. In order to survive, NKP had to offer high-speed, dependable service to long-distance shippers. Such service was very demanding on a railroad's locomotives, but the Nickel Plate's, 700-class Berkshires responded so well, that for years they passed the New York Central's, diesel-powered freights, as if

they were standing still. Their 69 in. drive wheels rolled seventy- and eighty-car, freight trains up to 60 and 70 mph over the flatland profile of the NKP, ably demonstrating the high-horsepower capabilities of 'Super Power'. Although the first fifteen of NKP's eighty Berkshires were built by Alco, the remainder, fittingly, were constructed by Lima, and one of these, No. 779, became the last steam locomotive ever built by Lima, when it emerged from the erecting plant in 1949. The Berkshire era came to an end with the retirement of NKP's 2–8–4s in 1958, but it enjoyed a revival a decade later, when No. 759 was removed from a museum to pull excursion trains for yet another four years.

What the advent of the 2–8–4 did for freight operations, the introduction of the 4–6–4 Hudson type did for passenger operations. The 4–6–2 Pacific proved that a locomotive with six, big, drive wheels could move like the wind. But, in order to maintain high speed over long distances with the longer and heavier trains of the 1920s, a locomotive required the steam-producing capability that the large firebox mounted above a four-wheel, trailing truck provided. Although six-

teen American railroads bought 4–6–4s, the most famous will always be the J-class Hudsons of the New York Central, that pioneered the wheel arrangement in 1927 and named it after the river that its main line followed in New York state. Soon after delivery, No. 5200, NYC'S first 4–6–4, pulled a twenty-six-car test train – weighing 1,696 tons – up to 75 mph. Further refinement was made after Paul Kiefer, the railroad's chief engineer of motive power, gained information in Great Britain in 1928 and 1929 about dynamic counterbalancing. Upon returning to NYC, he had all sixty 4–6–4s built up to that time cross-balanced, according to knowledge he had gained abroad. The Hudsons pulled the crack passenger trains of New York Central's 'Great Steel Fleet', which was led by the famous *20th Century Limited*. On the *Century*, one Hudson would usually run from Harmon, New York to Toledo, Ohio, – 621 miles – making seven station stops in fourteen hours. As successful as the Hudsons were, and their number had increased to 225 by 1937, the railroad required a locomotive with even more hauling capability, while costing less per mile to operate. Kiefer returned to the drawing-boards

and developed a Super Hudson. American Locomotive built fifty of them – the final ten with a streamlined shroud. The new locomotive retained the same general dimensions as the first Hudson, but offered significant improvements: increased boiler pressure from 225 to 275; increased weight on drive wheels with little overall increase in engine weight; and pistons, piston rods and crossheads made from lightweight alloy steel. When tested against the older Hudsons, the new engines developed ten per cent more boiler horsepower and twenty-one per cent more cylinder horsepower – and burned less coal in the process. They displayed so much strength, that boiler pressure had to be reduced to 265 pounds to counter an incidence of bent rods.

The tender was not neglected. During the 1940s NYC perfected a method to scoop water at 80 mph from track troughs. Thus, only a small quantity of water actually had to be carried aboard the tender, and a monstrous bunker carrying forty-five tons of coal – enough for the entire Harmon to Chicago run – could be designed into new tenders. As excellent performers as the 275 Js were, they are best remembered for their graceful lines and handsome appearance. They have been called the most beautiful of all American locomotives.

The 4–6–4 and 2–8–4 were ultimate expressions of locomotives ideally suited for the respective job of moving passenger trains and freight trains. As wonderful as these Super Power locomotives were, railroad officials expressed a desire to operate a locomotive that could perform interchangeably and equally well in freight service and passenger service. There had not been a locomotive like that since the tiny 4–4–0s had reigned half a century earlier.

67 A Union Pacific No. 8444 with an excursion train on the main line west of Rock River, Wyoming. The great clouds of smoke are for the benefit of photographers. For cleaning purposes sand is filtered through the boiler flues dislodging carbon deposits which collect inside, and causing great billows of black smoke.

68 A Rocky Mountain 'Rocket' diesel locomotive pulling into La Salle Street Station, Chicago.

69 A Hudson locomotive 4–6–4 class J-3 No. 5433 used by the New York Central.

70 A streamlined 4–6–4 Hudson for the *20th Century Limited*.

73

71 A Union Pacific Mikado locomotive pulling a train from Fort Collins at La Salle, Colorado.

72 A Union Pacific 4–8–8–4 'Big Boy' at Cheyenne, Wyoming.

73 A Union Pacific Challenger type locomotive eastbound at Archer, Wyoming.

It was in the wide open spaces of the West that the great 4–8–4 was born: a locomotive that could haul twenty-five-car passenger trains one trick and eighty-car fruit blocks the next trick. Baldwin built the first one for Northern Pacific and the type name Northern was established. The 4–8–4 was too good a design to be monopolized by any single part of the country, and the wheel arrangement was too popular to be universally tagged with the name Northern. In other places the 4–8–4 was the Niagara, Pocono, Dixie, Golden State and Greenbrier, to name only a few. One of the finest expressions of the 4–8–4 still steams in this, the diesel age. In the autumn of 1971 Union Pacific overhauled 4–8–4 No. 8444, so it could perform in special excursion service for steam locomotive enthusiasts. When this locomotive was delivered from Alco as No. 8444 in 1944, she not only was the last of forty-five, 800-class Northerns built for Union Pacific, but the last steam locomotive of any type that the railroad ordered. Her tall, 80 in. drive wheels were specified for hauling the numerous mail-and-express trains, as well as secondary passenger trains, that UP ran from Omaha to Los Angeles and Portland in the post World War II years. When diesels later took over these chores, the 800-class engines displayed their dual-service capabilities by rolling long freight trains across the Nebraska prairie. Despite the tall drive wheels, 8444 has a tractive force of 63,800 pounds, thanks to a large boiler operating at 300 pounds pressure and a total engine weight of 490,700 pounds. Railfans riding the excursion trains powered by 8444 have clocked her on many occasions at more than 90 mph, and on at least one occasion she travelled over Sherman Hill, the imposing gradient between Laramie and Cheyenne in Wyoming, in less time than that scheduled for the crack streamliners pulled by five diesel units. These feats are pale in comparison to the reliable story, that one of these locomotives once reached, unofficially of course, 130 mph out on the high iron across Nebraska.

Union Pacific, the railroad so closely tied to the legends and romance of the American West, was responsible for operating some of the most legendary locomotives of all time – the Challenger and Big Boy types. The first Challenger was a high speed development of 'double' locomotives, that had been widely accepted on mountain railroads since their inception soon after 1900. Such locomotives used two sets of cylinders and drive wheels, set beneath an extra long boiler. To negotiate curves, the front set was made to swivel, while the back set was mounted firmly to the frame and boiler. Thus, such locomotives received the general description 'articulated'. As first developed, these articulateds had steam directed from the boiler to move the pistons in the rear cylinders, and then had the same steam piped into large, low-pressure cylinders to move the pistons connected to the first set of drive wheels. Such locomotives, also named Mallets after Anatole Mallet, the Frenchman who devised the high-pressure and low-pressure principle, were slow, powerful creatures. By the 1930s the Mallet was losing favour, but the concept of using two sets of six or eight drive wheels on one locomotive – particularly in the mountains – was more popular than ever.

Union Pacific's Challengers, introduced in 1936, achieved high speed with 69 in. drive wheels and a 4–6–6–4 wheel arrangement, with each of the four cylinders receiving fresh steam directly from the boiler. The 4–6–6–4s were an outstanding success (Alco built 105 of them for UP alone), but the great Western railroad wanted a locomotive powerful enough to take freight trains over the Wahsatch mountain range in Utah without the assistance of a helper locomotive. Alco and UP devised a wheel arrangement, 4–8–8–4, that helped establish the new locomotives as the world's largest. The machine was so impressive on the erecting floor that an Alco workman chalked the name 'Big Boy' on the smokebox door. The nickname stuck. Twenty were delivered in 1941 and five more came in 1944. Although designed for use across the Wahsatch, they peformed all along the UP's Wyoming division, and became a familiar sight on the slopes of Sherman Hill. What makes a locomotive the world's largest? These are Big Boy's statistics: engine and tender weight – 1,208,750 pounds; engine weight – 772,250 pounds; boiler pressure – 300 pounds per square inch; drive wheel diameter – 68 inches; tractive force – 135,375 pounds; length of engine and tender – 132 feet $9\frac{7}{8}$ inches. Roaring along at full power, a Big Boy could develop more than 6,000 horsepower, and in the process could consume 100,000 pounds of water and 22 tons of coal per hour!

If Lima was the scientist and innovator about steam, and if

Alco was able to place its circular builder's plate on the likes of NYC Hudsons and UP Big Boys, where did this leave Baldwin? In terms of quantity Baldwin was foremost, and in terms of quality Baldwin built a large, raw-boned type of locomotive that saw action in all corners of America and made special inroads in the West. Santa Fe was a big buyer of Baldwin power. Encumbered only with the restrictions of a 4 ft. 8½ in. gauge across the wide open spaces of the Southwest, Santa Fe boasted Baldwin 4–8–4s, that were the largest locomotives of their wheel arrangement in the world. Atchison, Topeka & Santa Fe's 2900-class weighed 510,150 pounds and exerted a full 66,000 pounds of tractive effort with drive wheels 80 in. in diameter. They were equally at home rolling the likes of the *Chief* or a potato train. As impressive as these 4–8–4s were, Santa Fe and Baldwin went one better – by placing into operation, first in 1938 and then again in 1944, a total of thirty-five 2–10–4 locomotives with drive wheels 74 in. in diameter. Although these 2–10–4s were freight engines, their wheel size surpassed that of many American passenger locomotives. Their giant boilers and overall locomotive weight (549,500 pounds) enabled them to exert a tractive force of 93,000 pounds, which nearly equalled the 97,000 pounds of UP's articulated Challengers.

The dominance of the steam engine was finished in America about 1950, although the greatest American locomotives asserted themselves for another five to ten years. All that is left today are park and museum survivors, plus several dozen, smaller locomotives used on short, tourist lines. A few Super Power locomotives, such as UP 8444 and Reading 2102, haul occasional excursion trains, but it remains for a Baldwin locomotive to carry the tradition of steam most often on special trains. Southern Railway, a large (6,000 route miles) system stretching from Washington, DC, to New Orleans, Louisiana, shrewdly uses the steam locomotive as a public relations tool. It maintains several old locomotives, but the star performer is a 1911 2–8–2 Mikado type, dressed in the green-and-gold colours the railroad fancied in its steam days. On most weekends of the summer and autumn months, No. 4501, the archetype of all American steamers, is busy rolling excursion trains through the South, acquainting a new generation with the thrill of the age of steam, and bringing back fond memories to another.

74 No. 759, of the New York, Chicago & St. Louis Railroad, nicknamed the 'Nickel Plate Road' was retired in 1958 and resurrected in 1968 for excursions by the High Iron Company. It is seen here on the turntable at Jim Thorpe, Pennsylvania.

In view of the fact that Europe and America not only promoted the birth and development of the steam locomotive, but ushered it to a peak of scientific efficiency and raw size, it would seem safe to say that the lands on the Pacific Ocean side of the world had little to contribute to the story of the steam locomotive. Right? Wrong! As railroading progresses into the decade of the 1970s, it appears that Asia and Australasia will write the final chapter to the steam locomotive story.

Begin with the case of Australia. Matched against a population that even today exceeds only 11 million people Australia was a vast continent of 2,967,902 square miles. Only railroads could have adequately linked the various population centres and the far-flung frontiers. At first, it was assignment enough, that the railroads bind the various agricultural and mineral-producing regions with the settlements and ports within each state. As each state expanded, its government-owned railroads – with not much more than cursory thought given to the day when unification of all railroads would be desirable – evolved into systems each of remarkably different character. This individual character prevailed even into the selection and operation of locomotives. Australia, with a number of notable latter-day exceptions, did not have the economic resources to build its own locomotives, and so it ordered designs from abroad. These designs reflected the practices of various builders in America and Great Britain. Thus the Age of Steam in Australia became a microcosm of the Age of Steam everywhere else in the world. In no other single country could the diversity be found that was such a mirror image of steam locomotive practice, as it prevailed around the globe.

The seeds of diversity were planted in the 1850s, when Victoria and South Australia built 5 ft. 3 in. gauge railroads and New South Wales placed into service a 4 ft. 8½ in. gauge railroad. The initial intention had been to adopt a uniform gauge, but through faulty communication and a series of misunderstandings, the two gauges came into existence. The picture was further clouded during the next couple of decades when Queensland, Tasmania, and Western Australia decided that they could not afford to build large-gauge railroads, and opted for cheaper 3 ft. 6 in. narrow-gauge lines.

The nature of the commodities carried within each state was also responsible for the diverse character of Australian locomotives, although this character took time to emerge. New South Wales Government Railways, Australia's major system with some 6,055 route miles, ordered its first locomotives – 0–4–2s – from Great Britain. New South Wales continued to order locomotives from British builders during the late nineteenth century and into the twentieth. These engines were characterized by long, smooth boilers, running-board skirts, open cabs, and later, Belpaire boilers, and they culminated in the ultra-successful, C32 Ten-Wheeler. Between 1892 and 1911, 191 were built by Beyer Peacock,

75 Three C32 class locomotives hauling an excursion train at Oceanview, New South Wales, Australia, 1966.

76 A 4–6–0 type passenger engine No. 3664 leaving Newcastle on the Newcastle to Sydney express. They were nicknamed 'Pigs'.

77 This 2–6–6–0 Mallet locomotive with a mixed train seen here at night near Tjitchalenka, Java, was originally built by the Dutch railroad for service in the mountain sections of Java.

78 A Victorian Railways R class Hudson locomotive with an excursion train bound for Melbourne at night from Winchelsea in 1967.

79 A New Zealand Government Railways class JA type 4–8–2 climbing Arthur's Pass in the Southern Alps.

and a few were among the last steam locomotives used in New South Wales. Baldwin of the USA also delivered some 4-6-0s and 2-8-0s to New South Wales, but about the time of World War I NSWGR began building its own locomotives or placed orders with Clyde Engineering of Australia. When a fast passenger locomotive was required to pull the heavier trains of the 1920s, the C36 4-6-0 was produced. Between 1925-8, ten were built by the railroad and sixty-five by Clyde Engineering. The design was even borrowed by the Commonwealth Railways, operators of the Trans-Australian railroad, a line completed across the arid, west central region of Australia in 1917 to provide a link with existing railroads and establish transcontinental rail routes. Beginning in 1953, the C36s were rebuilt with Belpaire fireboxes, an unusual firebox design (highly favoured by the few railroads in the world that extensively used it) distinguished by a square rather than conical contour, where the firebox joins the boiler on top of the locomotive. The 60 in. drivered C36s, known by the affectionate nickname of 'Pigs' for their short, blunt shape, emerged from rebuilding with a tractive force of 34,000 pounds and a boiler pressure of 200 pounds.

Clyde Engineering proved equal to the demanding task of designing and building a heavy freight locomotive for NSWGR in the late 1920s. Twenty-five 4-8-2s in 1929 and 1930 introduced the three-cylinder arrangement and mechanical stokers to the railroad, and to Australia's most industrialized state. The finest hour was yet to come. In 1938 plans took shape on NSWGR drawing boards for a bigger, faster express passenger locomotive than the C36. Because of World War II priorities, the first of the new C38 4-6-2 Pacifics did not arrive from the builder, Clyde Engineering, until January 1943. Four more were delivered by early 1945. The locomotives featured a thick skirting over the running boards, a long cowling over the top of a smooth boiler jacket, a Belpaire firebox, and a 'bullet'-shaped nose cone. Yes, the new class was streamlined, in tune with the prevailing, worldwide, industrial styling practices, that found many locomotives of that era appearing in streamlined dress. After the war – from 1945-9 – the NSWGR's own workshops built twenty-five more C38s. These retained the skirting of the first five but did not have the bullet noses or cowlings. Also after the war, the C38s were painted in a sprightly, green livery with red or yellow striping. When diesels began taking away the most glamorous assignments, most C38s were painted in a more mundane but functional black. The class was hand-fired, operated at 245 pounds boiler pressure (the highest in Australia), had 69 in. drivers, generated 36,200 pounds tractive force,

80 A New South Wales Government Railways Beyer-Garratt with coal train near Dubbo in the western part of NSW. These engines are the largest in Australia and still going strong.

81 A South Australian Railways locomotive class 520 4-8-4 at Adelaide. The engine is patterned after the Pennsylvania Railroad's class T-1. It was retired shortly after this night-shot was taken in 1966.

82 A Victorian Railways class J 2-8-0 locomotive with wheat train on the Warracknabeal branch line. The 'elephant ears' are in the German style on this Australian engine.

and often exceeded the authorized 70 miles per hour speed limit. The C38s were husky locomotives – but retained a suggestion of their British lineage. They gave the impression of showing what British locomotives would have looked like had they been transported to the wide open spaces and permitted to develop.

An old supplier of NSWGR steam, Beyer Peacock, returned to the scene in 1952 to furnish the first of forty-two, 4–8–4 + 4–8–4 AD60-class, Beyer-Garratt locomotives. The Garratt, named after inventor H.W. Garratt, is a unique style of locomotive designed to produce maximum possible, pulling power over lines with light rail or extreme curves. Two sets of drive wheels, at opposite ends of the locomotive, are used: one set is located under a fuel tank and the other set is situated under a water tank. The boiler is suspended between these two tanks. Therefore, the heavy weight of the boiler does not rest directly on top of the running gear as with conventional steam engines, but is distributed evenly along the entire length of the locomotive. Garratts with high-capacity boilers can be powerful locomotives, yet can travel over light rail, that would buckle under smaller locomotives with more concentrated weight distribution. Garratts also are articulated to negotiate sharp curves. Although most Garratts were used in Africa (Britain had only three and America none), Australia's AD60s were the largest – but not the most powerful – in the world. They weighed 264 tons, were 125 feet long, had 55 in. diameter, drive wheels, and exerted 63,000 pounds of tractive force. A few still were working near Newcastle, New South Wales, as late as 1972.

83

To the south of New South Wales, the state of Victoria's 5 ft. 3 in. gauge, Victoria Railways specified smaller motive power to serve the many, flat-land, branch lines that tapped the yellow wealth of wheat. The order for Victoria Railways' last, major, steam locomotive purchase went to Vulcan Foundries for sixty, J-class 2–8–0s, a high-boilered ungainly-looking affair that nevertheless battled diesels into 1969. The railroad's warmest embrace of the big-time steam era, however, came in 1941, when a home-built, 4–8–4, weighing 260 tons and producing 55,000 pounds of tractive force took to the rails. But H220, nicknamed 'Heavy Harry', was too big for most lines, and money did not became available to strengthen the lines that could accommodate similar machines. So the embrace became only a brief flirtation and today Victoria's solitary 4–8–4 rests in a museum at Melbourne. The locomotive that thus succeeded 'Heavy Harry' as the premier Victorian steam engine was delivered in 1951 and 1952. Built by North British Locomotive Co., the R-class 4–6–4s were seventy strong, and displayed a husky appearance that belied their modest statistics: 32,080 pounds tractive force; 210 pounds boiler pressure; and 73-inch drive wheels. Their appearance also belied their ancestry. Painted black with scarlet running boards and

84

83 Queensland Government Railways narrow gauge C17 class, 4–8–0 on the turntable in Ipswich, Queensland.

84 A new Zealand KB class, 4–8–4 on the turntable at Arthur's Pass.

85 This narrow gauge C17 class locomotive near Warwick, Queensland, is hauling ventilated poultry cars. Large numbers of these locomotives were used as standard freight engines until the 1960s.

running gear, and possessing large smoke deflectors, they would have been right at home on German Federal Railways – and reflected their Scottish heritage no more than whisky resembles Rhine wine.

South Australian Railways charted its own course in locomotive procurement in 1926, shortly after an American, W.A. Webb, took over management of the ailing 5 ft. 3 in. gauge railroad. The SAR began taking delivery of large-boilered, American-styled (but British built) 4–8–2s, 2–8–2s, and 4–6–2s. When business increased during World War II, SAR's Islington shops designed a locomotive that could operate on the light, 60-pound rail common to much of the system and that could still pull heavy, mainline passenger trains. The 4–8–4 wheel arrangement – the most popular in America at the time – was selected, but the tractive force of only 32,600 pounds would have been a sad joke on an American railroad for a locomotive with eight big drive wheels. However, when the Aussies had finished applying the streamlined shroud to the locomotive, it was apparent that the American heritage lived on in South Australia. Because the new 520-class locomotive of 1943 wore a giant yacht-like prow over the smokebox – a direct imitation of the prow that the famous industrial designer, Raymond Loewy, had created for the T1 locomotives of the Pennsylvania Railroad only the year before. SAR was not through imitating American practice: it became the first large Australian system to convert to diesel locomotives. Examples of the 66-inch-drivered, 520-class engines have been preserved for museum display and possible excursion operation.

That the only conformity on the Australian locomotive scene was non-conformity was further illustrated by the country's two, large, 3 ft. 6 in. gauge systems, the Queensland Government Railways on the Pacific Ocean and the Western Australian Railways on the Indian Ocean. In the 1960s Queensland Railways was still very much a frontier railroad, using light, single track to ply up and down the coast, and here and there extend inland to serve the cattle country. Two locomotive classes predominated: the C17 4–8–0 and the B18¼ (and BB18¼) 4–6–2. Although the C17

was introduced as late as 1920, and the last of 220 was delivered as recently as 1953, the design was a throwback to the golden era of turn-of-the-century railroading, when small engines and big men challenged the obstacles that nature placed in the path of the audacious railroads. Indeed, the C17s – with iron pilot, tall stack, and spartan boiler – would have been at home climbing the gradients of the Rocky Mountains on one of Colorado's legendary, narrow-gauge railroads or battling through jungle growth to open a new frontier in Africa. The Pacifics were introduced in 1926 and perfected all the way up to 1958, when one became the last steam locomotive to be built in Australia. Used in both freight and passenger service, the 4–6–2s presented a squat appearance and were painted green with red trim.

Two things simultaneously changed the nature of Queensland Railways: dieselization and the opening of new, heavy-duty lines to carry coal and iron ore for export to Japan. Virtually overnight the railroad arrived in the twentieth century.

Like Queensland, Western Australian Railways had a narrow gauge system, but the similarity ended there. WAR had long depended on coal traffic, and was ordering large 4–8–2 locomotives in 1943. In 1955 twenty-four, V-class 2–8–2s were purchased from Robert Stephenson and Hawthorne Ltd. of England. Packing 33,630 pounds of tractive force, the husky Vs were narrow in gauge only. As fine and as varied as Australian steam power was, the decade of 1960-70 witnessed its last, large-scale usage.

Whereas the 3 ft. 6 in. gauge played a supporting role in Australia, it was the 'standard' gauge of New Zealand's extensive 3,500-mile, rail system. New Zealand Government Railways operated many interesting locomotives, all the way from tenderless, tank locomotives to small 2–6–0s, 2–6–2s, and 4–6–2s, up to larger J-class 4–8–2s and K-class 4–8–4s. Thirty, oil-burning, Ka-class 4–8–4s ran in the North Island, and six, coal-burning Kb-class 4–8–4s were assigned to the South Island. The Ks had a tractive force of 30,815 pounds. In 1960 the steam locomotive dominated New Zealand railroading; in 1971 the last, few, active engines were retired.

Steam may be finished in the South Pacific, but the great land masses and island chains of Asia and the Far East promise to be the last stamping grounds of the iron horse. Just as tourists travel to the exotic shrines and temples of Japan, Thailand and India to behold the riches and splendour of the Far East, steam locomotive enthusiasts, like modern-day Marco Polos, travel to these same countries to locate and record the sounds and sights of the vanishing, black monsters. For the steam of the lands bordering the Pacific and Indian Oceans is a fascinating blend of the old and new, large and small, foreign and home-built. Something of the geography, heritage and histories of these countries can be traced by close scrutiny of the motive power rosters. The island of Java in Indonesia provides an example.

When railroads were built during the nineteenth century in what was then the Dutch East Indies, they followed the flat coastal plains and required only small, lightweight locomotives. In the twentieth century the twin ribbons of steel turned inland to climb towards the volcanic mountains at the centre of Java, and more powerful engines were required to conquer the two, three and four per cent grades. Small Mallet locomotives, 0–4–4–2Ts (the 'T' signifying that the locomotive carried its own water tank straddling the top of the boiler, and did not have a separate tender) were imported from Germany in 1907 and 1908. Additional, but larger tank locomotives arrived from overseas during the ensuing decade – this time from the home country of Holland as well as Germany. It became obvious that still larger – and conventional, tender-type – locomotives were needed. In 1916 Alco of the USA supplied eight, 2–8–8–0 Mallets, locomotives of impressive size, despite a guage width of only 3 ft. 6 in. Alco built twelve more in 1919 before the railroad returned to Dutch and German builders for its post-World War I orders of the 2–8–8–0 types. For good measure, light 2–6–6–0s were ordered from Swiss builders. The steam performed without incident until the mid-1960s when diesels from East Germany made inroads. The overthrow of President Soekarno, coupled with the weak foreign exchange situation that resulted from the dictator's ruinous, economic policies, delayed Indonesia's diesel-buying plans. Many of the old

Mallets continue to operate, and have become the last Mallet-type locomotives in service anywhere in the world.

India's claim to the railroad history book may be that it is destined to become the last country in the world to build new steam locomotives. Indian government plans called for the construction of new steam locomotives to continue at least into 1972. Depending on the status of new locomotive construction on the Chinese mainland, and barring other unforeseen circumstances, India's Chittaranjan Locomotive Works should be the last erecting hall to outshop a new locomotive.

India intends to rely on steam for many years to come. Part of the reason may be that the technology of the country is not ready for a fast conversion to diesel; and rapid import of diesels and diesel fuel oil would deplete its foreign exchange. Diesels gained favour throughout the world, because they required few people for maintenance and operation, and they burned less fuel than steam locomotives. Yet India needs to maintain employment for its millions of people, and this steam does (the railroad is India's largest employer), from the engineer's cab to the workshops to the coal mines.

From the different railroads that colonized India, two immense systems emerged: one, a broad 5 ft. 6 in. gauge and the other, a meter gauge. These railroads are operated by the Government, but are broken into regional authorities. Many miles of 2 ft. gauge track also exist, some privately owned. Although sixty-three, different steam locomotive classes are found on the broad gauge and seventy on the meter gauge, the most outstanding type can be singled out quickly. The broad gauge, WP-class 4–6–2 now numbers

86 Indonesia is noted for its extensive variety of locomotive classes from many countries including the United States, Japan, Great Britain, Germany and Holland. This 0–4–4–2T tank engine with mixed train is seen near Bandjar, Java.

87 A NZGRW Pacific leaving Springfield for Christchurch. In the background are the snow-covered southern Alps.

into the hundreds; it has been built by foreign firms such as Canada's Montreal Locomotive Works as well as by Indian foundries. It is the standard passenger locomotive and is distinguished by a bullet-nosed, streamlined appearance. The WG-class 2–8–2, a widely-used, freight locomotive, shares the same boiler and many parts with the WP.

For a reason that someday could be the subject of a fascinating study, the romanticizing of and public acclaim for the steam locomotive has occurred to the greatest degree in Anglo-Saxon, English-speaking countries. Although steam locomotive appreciation has spread beyond America, Australia and England to France and Germany, it is almost non-existent behind the Iron Curtain. In the free world, declining interest accompanies a falling standard of living and a shift to the countries of Latin and South America, Africa, and Asia. The exception to this geographical pattern is Japan. Perhaps it is the common bond of creative, mechanically-minded people, but in Japan the railroad is every bit the fetish as it is in America or England.

Japanese train-watchers have their own magazine, produce their own hard-cover books, and take pride in an industrialized talent that supplies highly-detailed, brass, locomotive models to the world. It is with special sadness, then, that the Japanese are currently witnessing the phase-out of steam traction on the 3 ft. 6 in. gauge lines of Japanese National Railways. In late 1971 the most popular locomotive in Japan was retired. The C62-class 4–6–4s were massive-looking machines that had devotees far beyond the the shores of Japan. Forty-nine of them were built in 1948 and 1949 to pull the country's limited, express trains. For years they carried the colourful, circular headboards that displayed the emblems or names of such trains as *Heiwa* (Peace), *Hato* (Dove), *Sakura* (Cherry), *Fuji* (Mount Fuji), and *Tsubeme* (Swallow). The locomotive and tender weighed slightly more than 150 tons, the engine was rated at 30,644 pounds of tractive force with a boiler pressure limit of 228 pounds. The drive wheels were 69 in. tall, a respectable height even for a standard gauge locomotive. Most important of all, they were a product of Japanese industry – not once, but twice. The C62s were built in 1948 and 1949, true, but they employed boilers from wartime D52-class 2–8–2s.

The most common steam locomotive in Japan is the all-purpose, D51-class Mikado. Japanese industry placed more than 1,000 of these 2–8–2s on the JNR between 1936 and 1945. The medium-size D51 represents a logical progression in size from the smaller D50 2–8–2 introduced in 1923. As was normally the case with any locomotive class spread over hundreds of examples, there were many modifications and sub-classes. Some D51s were built with semi-streamlined cowlings – or 'skyline casings' – over the stack and boiler top. Wartime versions were spartanized, and later rebuilt to conform to general class standards. D51s have 55 in. drive wheels, exert 37,410 pounds of tractive force, and should be among the very last steam locomotives in Japan to be retired.

The veil of secrecy is beginning to lift over the Chinese mainland. The story remains to be told of what American-, British- and Russian-built, steam locomotives still are in service. The first train-watchers to visit China will have a priceless experience, because China may well have the largest stable of steam locomotives active in the world today – and for some years to come. Yes, much of the story of the Asian steam locomotive remains in the future.

88 A D51 Mikado pulling a freight train in the snow, bound for Hakodate from Sapporo on the northern island of Hokkaido.

89 A C62 class, 4–6–4 at Sapporo. This was considered the largest and finest locomotive in Japan and was retired in 1971.

90 A C61 4–6–4 type passenger locomotive seen here at the changeover point at Taira, north of Tokyo, where steam engines take over from electric to haul express passenger trains from Tokyo to North Honshu.

6. DIESEL AND ELECTRIC TRAINS

At a time when the transition from steam to diesel and electric traction is apt to be taken for granted, it is easy to forget, that it is now over ninety years since Werner von Siemens gave the first practical demonstration of rail haulage with electric traction at the Berlin Trade Exhibition of 1879. Eleven years later, electric locomotives were already in everyday use on the City and South London tube railway, to be followed in 1893 on the Liverpool Overhead Railway, by the system now known as 'multiple units', which has the motors incorporated in the passenger carrying rolling stock.

During the same period, electric traction had been applied with enormous success to street tramways, with the result that, by the turn of the century, it was widely acclaimed as the ideal means of traction for all forms of urban transport – a view that inevitably led to the popular supposition that it would soon supersede the steam engine on suburban and main line railways. Some thirty years later, when diesel power made its tentative debut on main line railways, there were similar predictions, but in the event nothing of the kind happened, and it was not until the second half of the

present century that these later and more efficient forms of traction became a decisive challenge to the near monopoly of steam power.

The main reason for this slow progress was, that in a world where commercial interests are of paramount importance, technical innovations that call for radical changes in established practice and the existing patterns of investment are usually unwelcome. This was particularly the case with electric traction, which was seen as a threat to the supreme alliance of coal and steam as the source of all industrial power. Coal was of vital importance to the economy of all industrial countries, and its transhipment was a principal source of railway revenues. Therefore, any threat to the consumption of coal was construed by the railways as a threat to themselves, and by the same token they were strongly opposed to electrification and the use of electricity as a source of industrial power. Naturally in countries such as Italy and Switzerland with ample resources of cheap hydro-electric power and where coal had to be imported, these strictures did not apply, but in coal producing coun-

92

tries such as Britain the attitude of the railways was undoubtedly encouraged by a good deal of political support. Indeed, some of the subterfuges resorted to in order to constrain the popular clamour for electrification were almost Gilbertian. One instance that occurred in 1902 was the way the Great Eastern Railway countered the public demand to electrify its Liverpool Street suburban services by building a huge, ten-coupled, steam engine known as the *Decapod* – which effectively silenced the critics by accelerating a 335 ton train from rest to 30 miles per hour in less than thirty seconds. Having made its point the company then waited for the excitement to subside and then quietly dropped the matter – but the long-suffering commuters waited another fifty years before electrification put an end to their miseries.

Similarly, about the same time the London, Brighton & South Coast Railway, worried by a proposal to build a new electric railway from London to Brighton, that would do the journey in forty-five minutes, promptly busied itself with a series of tests, whereby it somehow contrived to get a train from Victoria to Brighton in just over forty-eight minutes, thereby proving that the rival scheme was unnecessary. But once again, public expectations were disappointed, and it was not until the line was electrified by the Southern Railway in 1933 that the promise of a fast, regular interval service was fulfilled.

But inevitably this negative attitude did *not* always prevail in competition with the rapidly expanding tramway networks, and there were occasions when it was deemed expedient to electrify some urban services in order to stay in business.

This happened on Tyneside as early as 1904, when, after losing a third of its traffic to the tramways, the North Eastern Railway electrified its branches north and south of the Tyne, using multiple units and a third rail supply at 600 volts DC. This was closely followed by the Lancashire & Yorkshire Railway in the Liverpool-Southport-Ormskirk area in 1904-9 using a similar supply system, and in 1909 on the South London Line of the London, Brighton and South Coast Railway, using high-tension, single phase, alternating current at 6,600 volts. This line had been badly affected by

91 The first diesel electric locomotive to run on any main line in Britain travelled from St. Pancras (London) to Derby and Manchester on 15 January 1948. This 1600 hp locomotive is seen here leaving St. Pancras.

92 Thomas Alva Edison standing in the cab of his electric engine, 1892.

93 The driver of one of the regulation steam trains surveys what was then the futuristic diesel light passenger unit at Euston Station, before it left on a test run, 1938.

93

94

95

96

97

competition from the London County Council (LCC) tramways, and prior to electrification, traffic had dwindled from eight to three million passenger journeys per annum. Soon afterwards it recovered to ten million, a fact that no doubt prompted the company to overcome its remaining scruples by rapidly extending electrification to a total of 62 route miles on other suburban services. The immediate success of this venture had its effect on the neighbouring London & South Western Railway, which began to electrify its suburban services out of Waterloo in 1915, using multiple units and third rail collection at 600 volts DC, and also on the London & North Western, which began the conversion of its Euston-Watford, Broad Street-Richmond services in 1914. At this stage, other companies might have taken a similar course, but the advent of World War I and its aftermath effectively checked further schemes for many years to come. In fact, during the twenty year period between the wars, apart from extensions to the London Underground, the only large scale electrification in Britain was on the Southern Railway, which from 1925 onwards proceeded to

electrify the whole of its suburban services on the 660 volt, third rail system, and in addition became the first British railway to carry out main line electrification – to Brighton and Worthing in 1933, followed by an extension to Hastings in 1935, and Portsmouth via Woking and Guildford in 1937. However, the immense success of this venture, which gave a seven per cent return on investment, did not stir the apathy of those companies north of the Thames, and in 1939 when electrification in Britain stood at just five per cent of the total route mileage – rather more than 800 of the 1,000 route miles concerned was accounted for by the London Passenger Transport Board and the Southern Railway.

Diesel traction was still a negligible factor, amounting to no more than a score of small, shunting engines and a few railcars, and steam traction was still responsible for virtually all freight working and at least seventy-five per cent of the passenger traffic. So much for the prophets who thought that electrification would be a walk-over.

Abroad, the overall picture up to the outbreak of World War II was much the same as in Britain, with the notable

94 A Victorian Railways passenger express train hauled by a B class 5′ 3″ gauge 1500 hp Co-Co diesel electric locomotive built by General Motors.

95 The typical styling of SNCF main line diesels is here evident – decorated in pale blue and white with chromium trim this AIA-AIA 2700 hp 68000 class locomotive at work on a cross-country route.

96 The Rhaetian Railway – a metre gauge Bo-Bo-Bo 2400 hp 701 class electric locomotive as used on the 1 in 29 gradients between Chur and St. Moritz, Switzerland.

97 An electric two-car set, called the 'Blue Arrow' on the Lötschberg Railway near Kandersteg, Switzerland.

98 Pennsylvania Railroad, train No. 115, the 'Executive', runs from New York to Washington, where a part of it is combined with another train and then continues as the 'Silver Star' to Miami, Florida.

exception of mountainous countries, where the availability of cheap hydro-electric power and the existence of long tunnels and heavy gradients provided conditions, where electric traction could be used to the greatest advantage. In this context, Switzerland is certainly a unique example, having practically no natural resources, but amply provided with water power, which has been put to such good use that by 1954 over ninety-seven per cent of the traffic was electrically hauled. Here the conversion from steam to electric traction was commenced in 1919 and the system chosen was single phase, alternating current at 15,000 volts and a frequency of $16\frac{2}{3}$ cycles. From the outset, locomotives were used in preference to multiple units, mainly to facilitate the working of the interchange of passenger and freight traffic with other countries, which is the Federal Railways principal source of revenue.

However with the possible exception of Austria, Norway and Sweden, it is unlikely that other countries will follow the Swiss example in electrifying its entire network. The main reason being the initial, high cost of electrification, which in the absence of special reasons such as hydro-electric power or severe gradients, may have to be justified on purely economic grounds, such as a level of traffic density sufficient for the savings realized by electrification to balance the extra fixed charges. Obviously, on any given railway system only a percentage of the route mileage will fulfil this requirement – hence the reason why beyond a certain stage conversion is discontinued. In the case of the three countries we have mentioned, electrification has been extended to well over sixty per cent of the route mileage because of the exceptionally mountainous terrain and the availability of cheap power, but where these factors are of less importance, there is obviously a much stronger case for limiting electric working to fewer lines. In Britain a careful analysis has shown that thirty per cent of the main lines carry sufficient traffic to justify conversion, but this is probably a far too conservative estimate, since it ignores the fact that electrification invariably attracts additional business.

In the Netherlands, where cheap power is not available, it has been found practicable to electrify roughly fifty per cent of the route mileage, and to work the remaining half, which carries only about twenty-five per cent of the traffic, with diesel traction. Most of the passenger traffic is worked by diesel and electric multiple units, which for the relatively short distances involved, are ideal for the fast, regular interval, stopping services that span the whole country. Electric locomotives are also used on heavy, passenger services during the day and on freight services during the night.

Whether other European railways will eventually achieve a similar balance between diesel and electric traction is a

99 Liverpool Street Station (London) closed while two diesel electric locomotives pulling the wiring trains erect the overhead wiring in readiness for the electrification of the lines from Liverpool Street to Chingford, Enfield, Hertford (East) and Bishop's Stortford, 1960. 99

moot point. At the moment Italy, France and West Germany have all reached a stage, where electric traction on twenty-five to thirty per cent of the route mileage handles seventy-five to eighty per cent of the total traffic. This suggests that they may well decide, for the time being, that there is little scope for further electrification – except on a local scale. The fact that seventy per cent of a network carries only twenty-five per cent of the traffic is misleading, in that the greater part of these lines are essential feeder services into the trunk routes, and therefore have an overall importance, which some pundits, such as Dr. Beeching (at one time chairman of British Railways), overlooked.

It is in this sphere that diesel traction has mainly replaced steam in Europe, and it is on these secondary routes and branch lines that it makes the greatest saving compared with other forms of traction. Thus, the majority of European railways, including countries in the Soviet bloc, now accept as a matter of policy, that diesel traction should be developed as an ancillary to electrification – reserving the latter for intensive suburban services and main trunk haulage.

This does not necessarily apply to some of the minor countries, such as Greece, Denmark and the Irish Republic, which are sparsely populated and have insufficient industry to generate the kind of traffic flows that would justify electrification. In these cases diesel traction is the best solution and the Danish State Railways now uses it for ninety per cent of its traffic, while the CIE (Coras Iompair Eireann) in Ireland became the first nationalized railway company to achieve 100 per cent dieselization in 1958.

Outside Europe, a similar policy of balancing traffic requirements between diesel and electric traction is found in the USSR, where twenty-one per cent of the 90,000 route mileage is now electrified and carries fifty-five per cent of the traffic, with diesels mainly responsible for the remainder. A similar policy obtains in Japan, where electric working now extends to the thirty-four per cent of the total network, and also in South Africa, which has well over 2,000 route miles under catenary and is constantly extending the wire to cope with expanding traffics.

On the other hand, in the United States and its economic satellites, Canada, Mexico, Brazil and other South American republics, the situation is reversed, in that the diesel is undisputed king and electric traction the poor retainer. In fact, it is no exaggeration to claim, that there must be many people in North America who have never seen an electric train, since the vast majority of its railways, including the Canadian National and the Canadian Pacific are almost completely dieselized. This is all the more surprising, when it is recalled that America was a pioneer in electric traction, and that the Baltimore & Ohio was operating three main

100 A fleet of new diesel electric locomotives being prepared for a day's work at the LMS works at Crewe, 1936.

101 Denver & Rio Grande Western, No. 3079 bound from Salt Lake City to Pueblo, Colorado, climbing the Tennessee Pass. The Tennessee Pass was the original main line for the Rio Grande until the Moffat Tunnel was taken over in 1934. Today it accommodates freight service only.

line units as far back as 1895. By the turn of the century inter-urban railways, using electric locomotives and multiple units, abounded, but they went out of fashion with the streetcar, and few have managed to survive. Over a score of US railroads busied themselves with electrification in the early days – but almost invariably as a makeshift to do some job for which steam was unsuited, or as a stratagem – as when the B & O electrified its tunnel section under the Patapsco River in order to overcome municipal objections (based on atmospheric pollution). Occasionally it was forced upon them – the best known instance being when the New York legislature compelled the New York Central to discontinue steam traction south of the Harlem River after 1 July 1908. On the Norfolk & Western and the Virginian, electric working was resorted to for getting 6,000 ton coal trains over the Appalachian Mountains – but over thirty years later, when the Norfolk & Western made a re-alignment of the route on easier gradients, the electrics were replaced by steam. Only two major companies in the States ever took electrification seriously. The Pennsylvania and the Chicago, Milwaukee, St. Paul & Pacific with 672 and 662 route miles respectively. At its peak, the electrification of American railways reached the modest total of 3,100 route miles – a mere 1.23 per cent of their aggregate – and today that figure has fallen to 1,900, which is rather less than that of Spain.

Given the unified control of Federal ownership, the situation might have been very different, but fragmented by the self-interest of scores of independent companies, American railways were never in the running for large-scale electrifi-

cation on a coast to coast basis, if only because the cost of stringing catenary over such great distances was not only prohibitive but lacked appeal, since the density of traffic over most routes was not enough to warrant the outlay – which at best meant investing huge sums of money for long periods at a low rate of return.

Coincidently a solution was found in the diesel electric locomotive, which was first pioneered in America on a tentative commercial basis in 1925 by the firms of Ingersoll-Rand and General Electric. For a decade, production was almost entirely limited to 300 and 600 hp, shunting units of the twin bogie 'box-car' type, with a cab at each end, and later by 'hoods' with a single cab somewhat elevated above the rest of the superstructure. It was not until 1937 that bigger line service units of up to 1,800 hp began to appear. But when they did, the reliability of the diesel electric and its ability to cut costs relative to steam-working was already quite well established, and but for the intervention of World War II, there is little doubt that the replacement of steam would have been more rapid than it was. But even with this interruption, about half the total rail traffic in America was being handled by diesel electrics in 1950, and by 1960 they were virtually supreme on all lines except the few that retained some electric traction. Today there are more than 27,000 units of this type at work, and with the exception of commuter lines they handle about ninety-five per cent of the traffic. Undoubtedly, the enormous success of the diesel electric, both within America and as a worldwide export, has led to the policy of American builders to standardize on rugged, moderately powered units with medium speed en-

103

gines. Mostly in the 1,000-2,500 hp range, this type of unit is regarded as the ideal workhorse, because of its reliability, ease of maintenance and flexibility, since any number of units can be used together to make up the requisite horsepower to operate a given train.

It has often been claimed for diesel electric traction, that it gives every railway a stake in the benefits of electric traction without recourse to the crippling costs of overhead or third rail current collection, but quite recently some American railways have begun to question if that stake is enough, or whether straight electrification might not be a better proposition. The reason for this change of heart is, that in recent years competition has driven them to introduce much faster freight schedules, which have vastly increased the cost of diesel working. More speed simply means more horsepower per train load, and whether this is achieved by extra units or bigger units, the result is higher fuel bills and maintenance costs that spiral in direct proportion to the wear and tear of high-speed operation. The only way out of this dilemma is to produce more power at a lower cost, and given the requisite traffic flows (which, following the recent spate of mergers, is now a distinct possibility) electrification could be the right answer.

With examples like the success of Japan's electrified Tokaido line, and the fact that every other highly industrialized country in the world has chosen to electrify its main lines, there can be little doubt as to what needs to be done. Moreover, recent techniques – for instance, the direct use of industrial current in conjunction with silicon rectifiers – have actually reduced the cost of such schemes by at

least thirty per cent. But whether American railways have the morale and the means to tackle the problem is a moot point, all that can be said with any degree of certainty is, that if they fail to do so, their whole future will be gravely impaired.

Superficially, it may appear that the same argument could apply to Australia, where the replacement of steam by diesel electric traction is now in its final phase. But in reality, the situation is very different, because the country is still far too under-developed to warrant electrification, and the fact that the railways are government owned, should ensure that it will be done when the time is ripe. At present, only the New South Wales and Victorian Government railways have embarked on electrification schemes, and most of this is confined to suburban lines in the vicinity of

102 The SNCF 'Quadricourant' – a four-current express locomotive able to operate over four different voltage systems, designed for heavy fast trains and the Trans-Europe-Express (Paris-Brussels).

103 One of the ubiquitous DB class V200 B-B 2000 hp diesel hydraulic locomotives about to leave Hamburg (Germany) on an express run to the south.

Sydney and Melbourne. Altogether, the electric route mileage amounts to a little over 500 miles, which is about two per cent of the total Australian network. Most of the working is by multiple units, in addition to which there are about 100 electric locomotives for main line duties. The system used is 1,500 volts DC with overhead current collection. Diesel practice follows that of America, the majority of units being in the 1,000-2,000 hp range, although in Western Australia, where there is a lot of heavy mineral traffic, there are units of 3,300 hp. The Queensland, South Australian and Victorian railways also make considerable use of diesel railcars and trailers, which are ideal for working their many, lightly trafficked, branch lines.

In Britain, the replacement of steam by diesel traction was concurrent with the introduction of the £1,200 million Railway Modernization Plan announced by the British Transport Commission in 1955. The undue emphasis on diesel rather than electric traction contained in the Plan was explained as an 'interim measure' – but in fact it was government policy, intended to keep the steam-orientated, British Locomotive Industry on its feet by giving it a stable home market for diesels, to help it compete in this field for exports.

The result was a bonanza for the industry, and within a decade British Railways was in possession of more than 4,000, multiple unit vehicles and nearly 5,000 diesel locomotives – the latter comprising some fifty, different classes with a choice of mechanical, hydraulic and electric transmission systems. It was small wonder that there were endless teething troubles, and that, despite the excellent performance of the 'Deltics' on the East Coast main line, diesel traction in Britain has acquired a poor reputation for reliability. Much of the blame for this must attach to the haste with which it was done, often with untried equipment and before the proper maintenance facilities had been established.

On the other hand, post-war electrification has been eminently successful, precisely because each scheme has been planned and introduced in carefully phased stages.

The first two to be carried out after the war – between Manchester and Sheffield via Penistone, and on the London suburban route from Liverpool Street to Southend – were equipped on the officially recommended 1,500 volts DC system, but following the successful results achieved by the French National Railways with 25,000 volts AC, industrial current between Valenciennes and Thionville in 1954, the latter system was adopted as standard for British Railways, except on the Southern Region, where it was much simpler to extend the existing 750 volts DC, third rail network.

The paramount advantage of the high voltage system is that it permits a substantial economy in materials – the overhead contact wire is smaller in section, and therefore lighter than that required for DC systems, and there is a corresponding saving in the structures that carry the wire. Another advantage is, that it requires far fewer transformer sub-stations, and there is also a thirty per cent saving in the traction equipment. On the other hand, there is the disadvantage that the contact wire requires a greater clearance, and, as was the case in the Euston-Crewe-Liverpool-Manchester scheme, this can involve a very heavy, initial expenditure in modifications to the overline structures. On the final phase of this scheme – from Weaver Junction (which is north of Crewe) to Glasgow – the cost will be considerably less, as there are fewer bridges involved.

In addition to the Euston-Liverpool-Manchester lines, 25 kilovolts AC electrification has now been extended to the

104 Santa Fe's locomotive No. 39C enroute to Los Angeles with 'The Grand Canyon' passenger train at the summit of Raton Pass in New Mexico.

105 Canadian Pacific Rail's 'Canadian' at Stoney Creek Bridge, British Columbia, Canada.

106 The *Golden Arrow*, one of the comparatively few locomotive-hauled passenger services on the Southern Region hauled by a 2500 hp Bo-Bo electric locomotive with third rail current collection.

107 A typical Norwegian State Railways multiple unit at Oslo East Station on a local service and a 2200 hp class 11 Bo-Bo on a main line train to Bergen.

108 The *Brighton Belle* electric Pullman train approaching Clayton tunnel, 1962.

109 A 'Warship' class diesel hydraulic locomotive No. D829 *Magpie* approaching Reading with a down express, 1968.

110 Ore train passing between Mt. Tom Price and Dampier in Western Australia.

111 Western New York's severe winter weather doesn't daunt New York Central's No. 2881, a locomotive running from Buffalo to Albany.

Liverpool Street-Clacton-Walton-on-the-Naze service over the old Great Eastern main line to Colchester, to the Glasgow and Liverpool Street suburban services, including the former 1,500 volts DC line to Southend, and over the London, Tilbury and Southend lines out of Fenchurch Street to Shoeburyness. Work currently in progress is on the LMR main line between Weaver Junction and Carlisle, to be followed by the section from Gretna to Glasgow, and the recently authorized suburban services out of King's Cross.

On the Southern Region 750 volts DC system, the principal post-war extensions have been the Kent Coast electrification (1959-1962), covering all the main lines in the South East, and the Waterloo-Bournemouth services, completed in 1967 – making a total of 1,900 route miles, which is by far the largest, third rail network in the world.

The commercial results of these regular interval, electric services has clearly demonstrated, that this is the type of service that the public wants. In the first six months of the Kent Coast scheme the number of passenger journeys increased by twenty-seven per cent. On the Euston-Liverpool-Manchester services there was an increase of fourteen per cent in 1969, followed by ten per cent in 1970, and on the

Liverpool Street – Southend Victoria service an improvement of 126 per cent during the first ten years.

But electrification not only attracts business, it can do more work at less cost than any other tool the railway has, and with minimal harm to the environment. Moreover, it is perfectly suited to the techniques of automation, and in the long run it is this that will decide the issue in its favour.

112 A Swedish State Railway Ra class 3600 hp Bo-Bo electric locomotive introduced in 1955 for hauling the heaviest express trains.

113 The SJ class DM3 1–D + D + D–1. A 258 ton, 8400 hp triple articulated rod-driven unit built in 1960 for working 4,000 ton ore trains between Kiruna and Narvik in the Arctic circle, Sweden.

114 A new double-decker commuter train for Canadian Pacific Rail.

115 An Austrian Federal Railways 'Transalpin' express linking Vienna and Basle. The 3400 hp electric locomotive has a top speed of 93 mph and covers the difficult 580 mile journey in 11 hours 45 minutes inclusive of stops.

The idea of putting urban railways in tunnels underground originated in London some time in the 1830s. It simmered, fairly quietly, until 1851, when a scheme of Charles Pearson's to build a wide road from King's Cross to Farringdon Street, with six standard-gauge and two broad-gauge tracks in a tunnel below, was examined by a committee before being put to, and accepted by, the Common Council of the City of London.

Charles Pearson, City Solicitor, and John Hargrave Stevens, Architect and Surveyor to the City (Western Division) were the two men who fought hardest and longest to establish urban underground railways, and although Pearson's own scheme was cut and mangled by others, to emerge, a shadow of its original self, as part of an underground, mixed gauge line from Paddington to Farringdon Street via King's Cross, he was the undoubted father of the urban rapid transit, or underground railway. The railway which owed its origin to Pearson was London's Metropolitan Railway, opened on 10 January 1863, the prototype in style and name of 'Metros' throughout the world. Pearson himself died a few months before the line opened, but he must have lived long enough to see some of the work and to know that his brainchild was coming to birth.

After abortive trials by the Metropolitan's Engineer, John Fowler, with a specially built locomotive (*Fowler's Ghost*), which depended on hot bricks to keep up steam in the tunnels, so eliminating smoke, the Metropolitan was worked from its inception by Great Western Railway, broad-gauge locomotives and stock. These were banished when following a quarrel, the GWR withdrew its trains at short notice and forced the Metropolitan to borrow standard-gauge locomotives and rolling stock from the Great Northern Railway and rolling stock from the London & North Western Railway, until such time as the Metropolitan could acquire its own equipment.

The Metropolitan was a great success despite the smoke and steam. It was mainly a cut-and-cover line, built just beneath the surface, and was followed by the similar Metropolitan District Railway – intended as a partner but later, for a time, a bitter rival. These two cut-and-cover lines, greatly expanded, formed the main, sub-surface (as opposed to 'Tube') network of London Transport.

The first 'underground' to be built in Europe was 2⅓ miles long and ran mainly under one of Budapest's main thoroughfares. Opened in 1896, it too, was sub-surface. In the USA a Bill was introduced into the New York state legislature in 1864 to allow a 'subway' – or underground railway – to be built to the designs of A. P. Robinson. The Bill did not succeed, but when, from 1900 on, the main New York subway system was built, some of Robinson's routes were followed.

New York did have a subway, however, as early as 1867. It was only 100 yd. long and was built secretly by Alfred Ely Beach from the basement of a building on the corner of Broadway and Murray Street. Beach had permission to build two small tunnels, only 4 ft. 6 in. in diameter, in which to experiment with pneumatically-driven freight vehicles. But he ignored that, designed his own shield and built a 9 ft. diameter tunnel with a pneumatically-driven passenger car, which carried people up and down his little experimental line

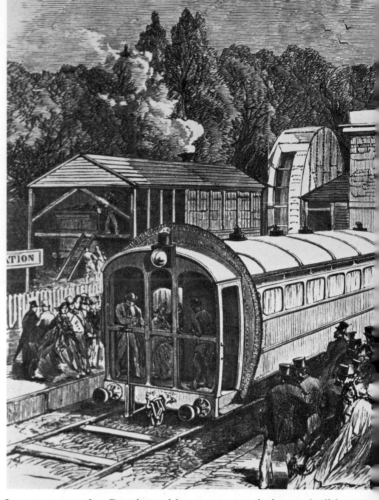

for some months. Beach could not get permission to build more deep subways, but he was given authority to build some subways for use by steam trains. These were never built – perhaps the success of Charles Thompson Harvey's 'subway in the sky' – the Elevated Railway – spoiled Beach's chances of success. The 'EL', though not an underground railway, operated in a similar manner on similar routes. Its incursion into the tomato-growing Bronx in 1886 at once extended the area of New York, and at the height of its career its steam-hauled and electric cars were carrying a million people a day.

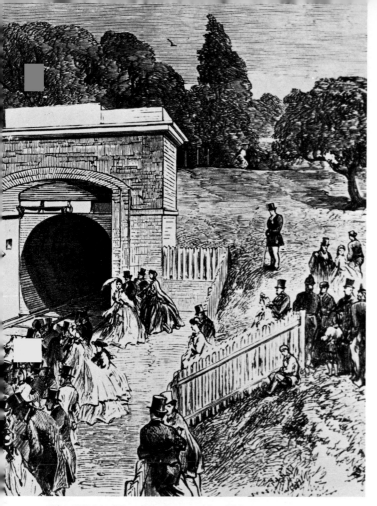

The 'EL' in New York – and in Chicago – set out to do the same job as that performed by underground railways from the beginning to the present day – to carry passengers swiftly under (or over) streets crowded with people and vehicles. Old photographs of most cities show clearly that the leisurely, horse-drawn days of the imagination were really nothing of the sort. The streets were packed with horse cabs, horse drays, horse buses, horse trams, horse everything, and congestion was as bad as, if not worse than, it is in the streets of today. For traffic engineering, except in a rudimen-

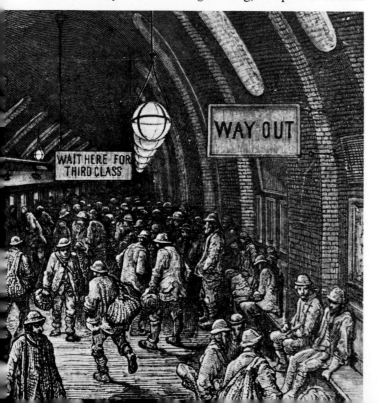

tary, rule-of-thumb style, was an unknown science.

What, then, does an underground railway offer, which makes it, though very expensive, so desirable, that every great city on earth either has one, is building or designing one, or is thinking (in varying degrees of urgency) about the need for having one built? The main reason is what it always was – the ability to move workers, shoppers, pleasure-seekers, tourists and all ordinary people engaged in their ordinary pursuits swiftly about congestion-free, private tracks under the heart of a city, ignoring what is happening on the roads. Then comes the second great point, that underground lines need take up no surface space (apart from staircase well-heads at stations). They can be built over and kept out of sight and, to the man in the street, out of mind. They are electric, so they cause no pollution. With modern equipment, at least 40,000 people can be carried in one direction in one hour – on some lines half as many again may be possible.

Motorways to carry this number (and more than fifty per cent of commuter-hour motor-cars tend to contain only the driver) would need so many lanes that they would spread into a concrete tangle, stifling the life from any city, as planners in the very home of the motor-car – the USA – have now come to realize. On a more personal level, you cannot read the news on the way to work in your own car, but to the average commuter, adept at folding his newspaper, it is simplicity itself when riding in the train – and, while you read, the train keeps going, when snow, fog and traffic jams turn the world above into a driver's nightmare. By its unobtrusiveness, the underground can save the historic centre of a tradition-steeped city and still give access to all its delights.

Undergrounds are not always underground. The modern tendency is to dive underground in the congested centre and then rise, possibly, to an overhead structure for the section immediately beyond the centre, running down to ground level, as soon as the lie of the land permits.

Only about a third of London's Underground is actually underground (including the characteristic, but unusual, deep tubes built in that ideal tunnelling medium, the London blue clay) and San Francisco's new seventy-five mile system for the Bay Area will have only just over a quarter below ground (or water, since there is a four-mile tube on the bed of the Bay). One of the best of the new ideas – seen in Chicago, San Francisco and Japan, for example – is to run the tracks in the median strips of motorways.

Underground railways exist very largely to carry considerable numbers of people into cities in the morning on their way to work and out again in the evening on their way home. For this task they need a full complement of trains, stations designed (especially in the central area) to pass great numbers of people through quickly, and a considerable staff. Before,

116 Seven Sisters Station on the new Victoria Line, London, showing a southbound train.

117 With the Metropolitan Railway only a year old the first attempt was made at what later generations called a 'Tube'. Already the Pneumatic Dispatch Company was carrying mailbags. In 1864, at the Crystal Palace, this trial was made with a full-size passenger line, with the car puffed through the tube like a pellet.

118 Workers crowding to get on the underground train, 1875. Print by Doré.

111

119

119 Ex-Metropolitan Railway 2–6–4T No. 114 at Amersham, 1938.

120 A view of St. Paul's and 'The Times' office from the underground at Blackfriars Station on the District Railway, 1875. Note that the artist has omitted one rail of the crossover.

between and after these peak hours it would probably, in most cities, be possible to use only half the trains, half the staff and much smaller stations to deal with the greatly reduced volume of traffic. One cannot, however, bring men and women to work for three or four hours in the early morning and then send them home until they are needed again in the evening – or only to a limited extent. It is this contrast between peak and off-peak services, with the need to build and supply everything to cater for a maximum number in a short period of time, which makes not only underground railways but all forms of public transport operation expensive – a steady load throughout the working day would make things much easier.

To carry these loads the use of clean, smokeless electric trains is now virtually universal, at least on in-town sections of lines, and nearly all railways use cars with steel wheels running on the familiar steel rails. In Paris, however, experiments were carried out in the early 1950s with rubber-tyred trains and Line 11, which runs from Châtelet to Mairie des Lilas, was fitted out completely for this stock by the end of

1957 and three lines now use these trains. The track is rather complicated, as are the wheel arrangements. Briefly, the rubber tyres run on two concrete beams laid along the tunnels, the tyres being kept on the beams by another, horizontal set of pneumatic-tyred wheels, which run on guiding rails or beams at the side of the track. At points and switches where the trains have to transfer from track to track, the side guides cannot be kept continuous, so there are standard-gauge, steel rails laid all along the tunnels next to the concrete beams and there the flanged steel wheels are mounted co-axially on the cars with the rubber-tyred wheels. At points the concrete beams fall away and the train runs over normal, rail-type switches on its flanged wheels. Should a tyre burst in normal running, the axle concerned will drop only until the steel wheel reaches the steel rail below and the train can carry on.

In tunnels, this rubber tyre has certain advantages of adhesion and – some say – of noise reduction, but the improved adhesion also demands more power and therefore produces more heat to disperse, so that the tunnels tend to get

hotter and hotter and need better ventilation or cooling. In the open air, where frost and snow can cake the running surfaces, the pneumatic tyre is at a decided disadvantage. In Paris, the latest stock to be ordered is once again steel-wheeled although another conversion has now begun. Nevertheless, the system has spread, under French influence, to Montreal, Mexico City, and now, Santiago.

Other types of underground railway are possible. For light work there is an American system – so far not installed in any city but at a very advanced stage, in which small coupled or single cars with pneumatic tyres travel over a flat concrete track on which they are guided by wheels running horizontally on each side of a central rail. Thoughts are also turning in the USA to long distance, high speed tube lines with some form of pneumatic propulsion.

Monorails are sometimes claimed to be suitable for underground railway work, and they could be so used for the short centre section of a monorail line, the rest of which is on the surface, but the monorails' special rail(s) and equipment would involve making the tunnels much bigger (and therefore more expensive), so their use is unlikely.

With modern materials, it might be possible to go back to the pneumatic propulsion system advocated in Britain by Brunel, among others, in the 1840s, but electric propulsion is so advanced and efficient that changes seem unlikely – except for the possible adoption of transistorized control for the motors, with which experiments are going on all over the world. The linear motor, a most important development because of its lack of moving parts and consequent frictionless drive, would seem at present to be more suitable for high speed main line or specialized cars than for an underground railway.

Comfort on trains is a matter of several trends going in different directions at the same time. In smaller cities, or those with underground railway networks of limited size, only basic passenger comforts tend to be catered for – e.g. somewhere to stand with a support to hold, heating and lighting. Newer, longer-distance lines, however, have more comforts, and in the USA where the problem is not only to carry passengers but firstly to lure them away from their private motor-cars, a high degree of comfort and air-conditioning are considered vital necessities. In other cities, with medium to busy routes, the aim is to give a fair number of comfortable seats which will accommodate most of the travellers in off-peak hours and passengers have to accept that

in the central area, at least in the peak hours, half or more of them will have to stand, and this, like many compromises, is probably the most sensible solution. The need for air-conditioning depends on the ambient temperature of the city served. A totally-underground line in moderate climates can probably be kept at an acceptable temperature by tunnel and station ventilating equipment without any need to air-condition the trains themselves. The problem, since electrical equipment and passengers themselves generate quite a lot of heat, is more often to remove heat than put it in. The picture changes considerably, of course, if in-town sections in tunnels are short and the trains spend much of their time in the open air. The problems then become much the same as those of main line railways in the area – and, indeed, of architects, builders, shop-owners and all others responsible for premises or vehicles used by the public. If there is general acceptance of air-conditioning as a commonplace of life in a given city, an underground railway must fall into line if it is to fulfil its purpose. Air-conditioning means much more than heating. It also means cooling when needed and a reasonable amount of humidity control.

Any modern, underground railway which is deeper than a few feet below the surface must have banks of escalators to take passengers up and down to platform level. Long

flights of stairs discourage passengers, as does the 'block' movement with spells of inactive waiting time, associated with lifts. The 'no-waiting' aspect of escalators is an incentive to travel, as are the bright, well illuminated, functional but attractive stations, which are a feature of modern systems and are recognized as an ideal to be achieved as quickly as possible in the modernization of other lines. Stations are designed today with the results of passenger-movement studies at hand, so that even walking flow is made continuous by the presence of adequate widths of passageways and stairs. At busy periods, closed-circuit television helps with crowd control.

Another delaying factor for passengers which must be overcome is that entailed in buying tickets. The sensible, regular commuter buys himself a season ticket, thus saving both time and money, but the casual traveller, or anyone who does not use a regular daily route, must buy his ticket somewhere – usually at a station ticket office – where he is likely to have to queue, or from a machine for which he either needs the right money or coins for which the machine will give change. On systems with flat fares automation to save ticket delays is easy. The only necessity is to make sure that a passenger pays that flat fare. In the simplest method he does so by dropping a coin into a slot to release a turnstile.

Because coins can be bent and jam machines, an alternative is to ask him to buy a ticket – or more often a number of tickets – which will operate the machine. Tickets of this type are often bought from booksellers, tobacconists, etc., rather than a railway office and it is only necessary to put one into a suitable gate mechanism to have the gate opened for access to the trains. Such tickets can have punched holes, codes, magnetic backings, metallic tape insertions, or quite a number of other identification points which will enable the gate to recognize them. With flat fares it is not necessary to check outgoing passengers. When a system has a large number of graduated fares, and many different types of ticket, a much

121 Train on the Hammersmith & City line at Hammersmith in the 1860s. Note the dual – broad and standard – gauge tracks.

122 The New York City automated subway train enters Times Square Station. Electronic devices on the posts at lower right help control the train's speed as it approaches passenger platforms. On non-automated trains the operator sits in a small compartment at the front, looking through the window next to the door.

more sophisticated form of coding, generally involving punched holes or coded magnetic backing, is required, and the gates need a considerable 'memory' system to recognize them all. Because of the complexity, tickets for such a system can rarely be sold by anyone but the underground railway itself and the scope for buying in advance is limited. In systems like this, tickets must be checked at the beginning and end of the journey. Apart from the season ticket, the best, time-reducing possibility for such railways is the 'stored-fare' ticket, which may cost, say £2.00 or £4.00 (or any other figure according to individual needs). When such a ticket is put into a gate to open a way to the platforms, it is impressed by the gate with coded information giving the station name, date, etc. At the destination the outgoing gate 'reads' this information, calculates the proper fare, deducts it from the total and returns the ticket, now worth the price of the journey less than when purchased. The value remaining in the ticket can be checked by putting it into a 'reader' which will display the value in hand. Such tickets are the subject of much experiment and may one day be the ideal ticket for underground railways which have a common fare structure with the city's buses, trams, ferries, etc. It could be used on any of them and, unlike the season ticket, requires no pre-selection of route. It could be a great timesaver.

The other main field of underground railway automation today is in automatic driving. There is a tendency to think that automatic driving of trains is in itself a good thing, but this is only partially true. It does enable all trains to be driven in a standard manner – the best manner – and thus saves current and evens out running-time fluctuation due to indivi-

dual styles of driving. But its main use is to enable a train to be operated either without a crew or with only one man on board who, freed from driving duties (though a qualified driver for emergency purposes) can concentrate on other aspects of running the train, such as opening and closing the doors at stations (helped by closed-circuit television to see the parts of the platform obscured from direct vision by passengers) setting the automatic driving equipment into action, monitoring the performance of the train, driving it into and out of the depot and reversing it at the journey's end, as well as making announcements to his passengers if needed. Most, if not all, of these functions could be performed automatically or by some source outside the train. For example, a man on a station platform could close the doors and start the train on its way and open the doors of the next train from external switches or by inductive controls from a platform console, but the many underground railways which are experimenting with or adopting automatic driving agree that despite automatic lifts and other unattended equipment, passengers as a whole are not ready for completely unmanned

123 Wembley Park Station in 943 showing a Metropolitan train bound for Aldgate on the far side, with two Bakerloo Line trains in the foreground. All the trains are made up of prewar rolling stock.

124 The new east-west underground Regional Express line in Paris. This line uses limited stop, fast trains of main line size to give rapid journeys across Paris. It is linked to the Métro at stations so that journeys can be begun or ended by using the Métro with its closer-spaced stations and more extensive network.

125 A functional but still attractive station (Rehberge) with a Tempelhof-bound train on the Berlin underground railway.

trains. Especially in the case of two-track tunnels where access to a stalled train is easy, however, there seems no reason why this should not come.

Automatic driving can be achieved by two methods. In one – adopted in London – local trackside controls give coded instructions to trains about the safety aspects of the track ahead, controlled by feed-back from the last train to pass, while other trackside controls, carefully positioned after theoretical and practical tests, tell the train where to start coasting and where to brake to travel at a pre-selected speed and finally to stop in the right place at the platform. The other main system, used in San Francisco, gives continuous feed-back of information from all trains to a central computer, which issues instructions to every train when to start, what speed to run at, and so on. There are numerous variations, including trains with on-board computers, which give instructions to the train according to a preset programme when the train has travelled pre-arranged distances.

This short chapter can only touch the fringe of the possibilities of underground railways for passengers, but the world as a whole is experiencing a great upsurge of interest, with dozens of cities – in Europe, the United States, Canada, Central and South America and Russia, where underground railways are already well established, as well as Australia, New Zealand, China, and other countries where such railways are new – preparing to join the list of those which already have underground systems. Soon it may well be truly said that the underground or rapid transit railway is the hallmark of a great city.

126 New York. A New York-bound train from Newark of modern cars on the Port of New York Authority's Trans-Hudson system (PATH) entering Harrison Station.

127 Chicago has made a feature of running some of its newest lines in the median strip of motorways. This train is approaching 69th Street Station on the Dan Ryan route, with four lanes of motorway on each side of the tracks.

128 London. The train operator's cab in an automatically-driven London Transport Victoria Line train. The operator's seat is folded against the rear wall in this view. Controls for manual operation when necessary are mounted on a neat desk, which also carries a display showing the safety-signalling code in operation at any time.

129 The impact of a new subway system on an existing city. A cutaway view of Powell Street Station on the San Francisco Bay Area Rapid Transit District line (BART), expected to open in 1972. The BART trains are at the lowest level with the municipal (streetcar) platforms above and the concourse just below the road level.

130 A stainless steel car working on the Market-Frankford subway/elevated line in Philadelphia. They are forty per cent lighter than the cars they replace, about one-third roomier (fifty-six passengers) and considerably faster (maximum speed 55 mph).

131 San Francisco. One of the luxury trains built for the Bay Area Rapid Transit District's new railway system – part underground, part at ground level and part elevated.

132 The interior of a BART car, with carpeted floors, wide tinted windows, well-upholstered seats, temperature control and new style of lighting. Each car seats seventy-two and BART is expecting to be able to give all passengers seats, even in rush hours.

8.
FREIGHT TRAINS

There's a deep sense of romance about the freight train, romance compounded of many-coloured box-cars, hoboes riding the rods in hopes of finding their El Dorado, smoking stoves giving an unexpected touch of domesticity in a lonely brake van or caboose. Few people stop to question what is in those box-cars or why; the freight train for many is simply a part of the landscape.

The archetypal freight train conjured up by the mind is a mixed collection of vehicles with loads in great variety. Coal in open wagons, refrigerated vans for foodstuffs, oil and tar

133 This giant new railroad car, designed to carry thirty subcompact automobiles by hanging them nose down on side panel-ramps, is the product of a joint research effort by Southern Pacific and General Motors.

in sombre coloured tanks, livestock in rows nosing through the bars, brightly painted, farm machinery lashed down on a flat wagon, steel girders chained securely to purposeful bolsters. At wayside stations the train is divided, shunted; wagons are left behind and others taken on. The freight train goes on its way.

Twenty years ago, it seemed that this would always be the way. True, there were improvements and innovations, some of them far-reaching. Diesels were nudging steam power out of the way and making it possible in some cases to operate longer, heavier trains. Steel and aluminium were taking the place of timber in wagon construction. In Britain, where a large proportion of the freight rolling stock was fitted only with hand brakes, progress was made in equipping wagons with continuous brakes, so that they could move faster.

But in principle the movement of freight had changed little since the days when the railways had first become established as common carriers, accepting and delivering at innumerable city and wayside freight depots, whatever customers chose to send, provided it was within the limits of size and weight, and was not offensive or dangerous. In many parts of the world, where roads have not been extensively developed, this is even now the case.

Elsewhere, however, competition from road transport has been growing since the 1920s. World War I played a major part in this, both by encouraging the development of motor transport and by enabling many subsequently to enter the haulage business using war-surplus vehicles. These operators could pick and choose their loads in a way which the railway as a common carrier could not; they could also offer a personal, door to door service, which was attractive to the customer, often at rates which undercut those of the rail service.

134 Coal traffic is an important factor on the Indian Railway. The train of high capacity wagons is leaving the Singareni Coalfields.

135 A fully loaded wheat train en route to Geelong on Victorian Railways during the record wheat harvest of 1960-1. The picture shows a North British-built N class 2–8–2 No. 499 piloting a Vulcan Foundry-built J class oil-burner No. 531 and a C class 2–8–0 No. 16 pushing up in the rear.

136 Train of mercy: New South Wales Government Railways transferred starving livestock to southern pastures during the 1946 drought.

136

In many countries it took some time before legislation caught up with this situation, and then it was largely concerned with such matters as safety standards and drivers' hours of working. Only in recent years has the sheer problem of road congestion turned the thoughts of governments towards encouraging greater use of railway freight services, either by protective legislation, or by giving railway administrations the freedom to compete commercially on the same basis as other transport operators.

Meantime, during the past forty years there has been an increasing tendency for the railways to be left with the freight that nobody else wanted to carry, for instance, coal and iron ore, impressive in weight and bulk, which requires vast fleets of rolling stock, yet not producing proportionately high revenue, or 'smalls' traffic of packages and consignments less than a full wagon load, but all needing a greet deal of labour in handling and documenting.

In Britain, France, Germany, in America, Australia, Japan and almost every other part of the world, country freight depots ambled through their daily work, their equipment less and less up to date, their consignments more and more being diverted on to the competing services. But their costs of upkeep and staffing still had to be paid, and were all the time rising.

Competition in some areas was so intense that railway branch lines were closed completely. Even in India, where road development tends to be localized, the Great Indian Peninsula Railway suffered such severe road competition on its branch from Agra to Bah, opened in 1928, that it was forced to close it in 1939. These problems were in many countries masked for a while during World War II, when petrol shortages and wartime needs threw an enormous traffic-load on to the railways. But once the period of post-war reconstruction was over, railway administrations and national governments began to take a hard look at the future of freight on rail, if not at the future of rail itself.

In Britain, some of the problems were historical. Competing companies had laid out the lines, and each had had its own stations and depots serving the same localities. Although these competing lines had been grouped into four main systems in 1923, and nationalized as one system (albeit with six semi-distinct regions) in 1948, there were until recent years still many towns where from two to half a dozen depots remained open, doing work which only demanded one.

This duplication of freight depots is much less common in continental Europe, where main line railways have mostly been State enterprises or confined to specific regions, and in Australia it occurs only at State boundaries. In North America, however, where railways have been and are still owned by competing companies, the multiplication of freight depots and yards reaches remarkable proportions. East St. Louis, for instance, is served by no less than thirty-seven freight yards. However interesting this kind of variety may be for the enthusiast, the cost of maintaining all these separate facilities hangs like a millstone around the neck of the railways' finances.

On British Railways, Dr Richard Beeching, at that time Chairman, was in 1963 the first to suggest a radical change

from traditional ways of handling freight. Until then, the basic unit of rail freight transport was thought to be the wagon. It was shunted in yards, detached and attached to trains as necessary to get it through to its destination. Dr Beeching pointed the way towards unit trains – trains which moved as a complete unit between loading and unloading, thus saving all the time and costs of coupling and uncoupling individual wagons. In particular he was concerned with what he called 'liner trains' – later known as freightliner trains – which would carry containers.

The container idea as such was not new. The idea of a box, in practice often shaped like the body of a railway van, which could be loaded at the customer's premises, taken on a horse drawn lorry or motor truck to the railway depot, transferred by crane on to a railway flat wagon for the main part of the journey, then taken by road again to its final destination, had appealed to many people over the past fifty years, for purposes ranging from household furniture removals to distribution of bread and biscuits.

But these containers had always been carried on individual wagons in ordinary trains. What was new about the freightliner scheme was the idea of a complete train carrying nothing else but containers, running between terminals specially designed and laid out for handling them. The first service began in 1965 between London (York Way) and Glasgow; today sixteen main centres are served.

137 A hump yard with retarders and classification tracks at Montreal. Freight cars passing through the yards that make up the terminal are weighed automatically, without stopping, on the scale immediately behind the crest of the hump, on their way to the forty-track classification yard.

138 Pennsylvania Railroad's famous GG–1 class with streamline design by Raymond Loewy was the most mechanically satisfactory and long-lived of the electric locomotives. Originally used for passenger service, they were later converted to freight. One of the class is shown here westbound with automobile train along the Susquehanna River.

it was
furthe
Sydne
existi

Th
using
tackle
almos
ways,
them.
of its
have
vehicl
avoid
retain
load.

Thi
has b
loadin
the h

143 French Railways has produced an ingenious solution known as 'Kangarou', using flat wagons with a depressed centre which can accommodate the rear wheels of a semi-trailer only a matter of centimetres above the rail, while the body occupies the same space a container would take up. In Germany, Switzerland and Austria, complete loaded lorries are carried on Dültinger low-floor wagons with sixteen wheels of extremely small diameter.

The dream of inventors down the years has been to produce a semi-trailer or lorry which would be equally at home running singly on the road or coupled in a train on rail. Although many versions have been tried, none has so far been a resounding success. One possible rival to the container in some spheres however, lies in the humble pallet – the framework of wood or metal which allows a fork-lift truck to insert its forks beneath a load. The rectangular, standard, ISO container does not make the fullest possible use of the railway loading gauge, whereas palletized loading of freight in ordinary railway vans does, and with far less cost in equipment.

Containers and piggyback have been the most spectacular developments in railway freight in the last ten years. Less apparent but just as significant has been the growth of other types of unit train, carrying one commodity over a regular route.

In the USA and Canada, trains of between seventy and 140 hopper wagons, each with a capacity of 100 tons of coal, circulate continuously between coal mine and power station on a number of routes. Loading is often carried out on the move, with the train of hopper wagons moving slowly through giant coal silos to receive a steady stream of coal. Unloading may be through bottom doors in the wagons and chutes between the rails, or, as at Detroit Edison's new Monroe station, by a rotary dumper which tips each wagon in turn without uncoupling it from the train; couplings are specially designed to allow this.

144

145

146

143 Union Pacific's No. 52, a 5000 hp locomotive known as a General Electric U50 type at Green River, Wyoming.

144 One of fifty 'T' class bogie wagons, specially built for conveying cattle by the inter-island ferry service, under construction at New Zealand Railways Addington Workshops, Christchurch.

·145 En route to the Continent; newly manufactured British cars on car wagons being loaded on to a British Railways Eastern Region train ferry.

146 The first train goes over Australia's first automated hump shunting yard, belonging to Victorian Railways, Melbourne.

147 Company trains: this block train of specially designed vans is really an extension of the assembly line as it carries car components between Ford factories at Dagenham and Halewood, England.

147

Trains serving this power station can be formed of up to 146 wagons, hauled by five diesel locomotives, two of which are 'slave' units located part way through the train and radio-controlled from the leading locomotive.

In Britain the name 'merry-go-round' was coined to describe unit train workings which ensure a continuous supply of one particular commodity. Merry-go-round working requires not only the use of unit trains, but provision of a large loop or circuit at each end of the journey, to permit continuous loading and unloading without time-wasting shunting of the train. At Northfleet near London, Blue Circle's recently completed cement works has an unusually complex merry-go-round circuit, carrying three commodities. A total of ninety trains a week bring coal and gypsum to the works and carry more than 26,000 tons of cement to depots as far north as Scotland.

Unit trains are used in many parts of the world, on specialist railways built to carry one product from a mine inland to a port for export. In Western Australia, where 1,000 miles of standard gauge railway have been opened in the past six years, three major lines of this type are hard at work and three more are under construction or proposed. Typical is the Mount Newman Railway, 265 miles long, which carries iron ore from Mount Whaleback to Port Hedland. Each day up to eight trains composed of 135 wagons of 90-ton capacity make the round trip to the coast and back.

This line is privately owned, but others, such as the WAGR standard-gauge line from Koolyanobbing to Kwinina, form an integral part of the existing network. Another line in this category is that from Kottavalasa to Bailadilla in India, which after five years of diesel operation is now to be electrified.

One result of British Rail's interest in the idea of unit trains has been the growth of the 'company train', one which carries raw materials or products for one particular company, or forms part of its internal transport by transporting parts from one factory to another. BR runs more than 1,600 company trains each week, carrying products as varied as fertilizer, liquid oxygen and motor car parts. Long-term contracts encourage companies to invest in this form of transport, and either to buy their own rolling stock or to lease it from one of several firms which will provide it, together with maintenance and repairs.

This swing back to private-owner wagons is interesting, because at the time of nationalization in 1948 almost all the then privately-owned wagons had been taken over by BR. These many-coloured wagons had been a feature of the railway scene in Britain, but many were of obsolete design and their presence made it difficult for BR to plan modernization of freight working.

148 A double consist bauxite train (with trailing load of 4,600 tons) powered by two R class 1950 hp English Electric diesel locomotives en route from Jarrahdale to Kwinana. This is one of the heaviest narrow gauge trains in Australia. The bauxite wagons have aluminium bodies and pneumatically operated bottom discharge doors.

149 Piggyback operation, with road trailers carried on rail vehicles, has found favour in North America, and in France where their version is called 'Kangarou'.

151

Long-term, company train contracts make it possible for firms to invest in rolling stock for their own specialist requirements; alternatively BR will supply special vehicles and even paint them in the company's own colours. Ford Motor Company's blue-painted vans, filled with automobile parts, shuttle twice daily between factories at Dagenham and Halewood; Shellstar's curtain-sided wagons, loaded with bagged fertilizer, run between Ince, Cheshire and eighteen strategic depots in agricultural areas; and block trains of steel bars move from Round Oak Steel Mill to Tube Investments' mill in Staffordshire.

Almost half the company trains on BR carry petroleum products. Shell-Mex & BP now has a fleet of over 5,700 rail tank cars in Britain, and of these some 850 are of the 100 tons, gross-weight types, which have been permitted on BR only in the last few years.

Most of these trains start and finish their journey in factories or depots belonging to the companies, and not to BR. Indeed, looking at the freight picture as a whole, more than ninety-five per cent of the consignments moving on BR today start their journey on private sidings, and ninety per cent of the freight is provided by seventy-five major customers. Thus, although in Britain as elsewhere there has been wholesale closure of wayside freight depots, there has at the same time been extensive development of sidings and specialized loading installations within the premises of the major industries.

In West Germany private sidings have been developed even more than in Britain, but the emphasis is not so heavily laid on unit trains. Some 15,000 firms have access to the German Federal Railway through private sidings, and eighty per cent of the system's freight passes over them. A large proportion of this is sent the traditional way in wagon loads, shunted from train to train, sorted in marshalling yards, and labelled and documented.

Thus, although in Europe the traditional wagon-load, freight train has tended to be overshadowed by new developments in containers and unit trains, it has still an important part to play. In other parts of the world, such as North America and Australia, it has as yet been scarcely challenged by the new ways of working. But work has been going ahead to make it more efficient, and in particular to link it with computers. Railways are a natural for computers, for only a computer can cope with the mass of tiny scraps of information – wagon numbers, loadings, restrictions, tonnages, shortages of wagons, etc. – which railway operation generates.

In North America, where about two million wagons are interchanged between the different railway systems, a programme has just been completed of labelling all wagons with a panel marked in reflective bars, which can be read by an electronic scanner at the trackside at train speeds up to 80 mph. This information can be fed back over telephone lines to a central computer to act as a basis for accounting,

152

timetable planning and the checking of progress of consignments. A similar system is being tested for European railways in Czechoslovakia at present.

Most wagon load freight passes through marshalling yards, where it is sorted into trains for particular areas or destinations. Important yards like Toton on British Rail, Mughalsarai in India or Hamm in Germany are major railway landmarks. Within the last year BR decided to spend £830,000 on modernizing New Yard, Scunthorpe, after an interval of five years since its last marshalling yard programme, finished in 1966.

Japanese National Railways has just completed modernization of a hump yard at Takasaki, an important junction in Honshu, which can handle 2,600 wagons per day on twenty-five classification tracks. Wagons uncoupled from the incoming rakes and pushed over the hump then roll by gravity and are controlled by four different types of retarder on the track. Points are set by computer.

Japan, like Britain, Australia and continental Europe, has a large number of four-wheeled wagons. In North America the double-truck or bogie wagon is virtually universal, and in Europe the changeover from side buffers and screw couplings to automatic couplers, now scheduled for 1979-81, is already giving a boost to purchase of bogie wagons. In Britain, the presence of archaic wagon-turntables for many years retarded development and there are still large numbers of short wheelbase, four-wheeled wa-

150 A colourful Canadian Pacific freight train emerging from the Red Sucker Tunnel, near Port Coldwell, Ontario.

151 Traditional loading methods give way to palletization in a Swiss Federal Railways freight department.

152 Eastbound freight on the Erie-Lackawanna Railway near Corning, New York on the Canaisteo River. The run is from Buffalo to New York City.

153 To permit this out-of-gauge load to be carried on German Federal Railways a special wagon straddling two tracks is used.

154 Virtually a portable siding: this German Federal Railway four-wheeled van is moved on a many-axled road vehicle through the streets of Duisburg to its destination.

155

155 A modern freight train crossing through New South Wales, Australia.

156 Cattle being loaded at Julia Creek in north-west Queensland for haulage of nearly 600 miles to coastal treatment plants. Queensland Railway hauls approximately three million head of livestock annually, including 1.3 million cattle and 1.6 million sheep.

157 A modern freightliner of Freightliners Ltd. (British Rail).

156

GLOSSARY

ENGLISH	AMERICAN	ENGLISH	AMERICAN
Signal box	Tower or signal station	Coaling road	Coal track
Breakdown vans	Wrecking trains	Sorting sidings	Classification tracks
Brake vans	Caboose	Reception sidings	Receiving yards
Locomotive shed	Engine terminal	Assembling sidings	Departure yard
Locomotive shed master	Enginehouse foreman	Neck	Throat
Goods trains	Freight trains	Double incline	Hump
Wagons	Freight cars	Down yard shunting	Switching tracks up
Vehicles	Passenger cars	Up yard shunting	or down to the yard
Axles	Number of axles in the train	Downtrain	From the home terminal
Bogies	Four-wheel trucks	Collieries	Coal mines
Foot plate	Deck of locomotive	Train examiner	Car inspector
Driver	Engineman	Line clear ticket	Ticket type of clearance cards
Regulator	Throttle		
Assistant locomotive	Helper	Pilot man	Individual who rides trains or locomotives without a staff or ticket in staff territory
Banker	Pusher		
Cross	Meet		
Loop	Passing track	Mail sorting van	P.O. car
Level crossing	Highway crossing	Line side	Along the right-of-way
Shunter	Yard or switch engine	Mail pick-up standards	Mail cranes
Shunting	Switching	Draw gear	Drawheads
Marshall yard	Freight yard	Guard	Conductor
Marshalling	Classifying	Brake sticks	Brake club
Engine road	Engine track to engine house	Express goods	Fast freight

160 British Rail locomotive No. 70002 standard class 7 for mixed traffic, 1951.

161 Southern Pacific's 4–8–4 locomotive built for service on their famous 'Daylight Trains'.

160

ENGLISH	AMERICAN	ENGLISH	AMERICAN
Empty coaching stock	Deadhead equipment	Shunting master	Switching foreman, sometimes hump foreman
Reception line	Inbound yard track		
Performing trains	Making up trains	Main	Through tracks or main line
Attaching vehicles	Picking up cars		
Brake cars	Express cars	Workshops	Shops
Ambulance boxes	First-aid kits	Detonators	Torpedoes (no fuses are used)
Crow	Peep of the engine steam whistle		
Sleepers	Ties		
Permanent way inspector	Roadmaster	Bank	Grade Grades are kept:
Fog signalman	A permanent wayman who is picked as fog signalman and put at fogging posts where signals cannot be seen during fog or falling snow		1 in 100 1% 1 in 50 2% 1 in 33 3% 1 in 18 4%
		In England there are no headlights or bells on locomotives	
Work rumpus	Work gang	Goods van	Car that the conductor rides in
Uptrain	To the home terminal		
Hours and minutes of departure from home terminal are usually used for down and up trains and not the engine numbers or train numbers		Wrong line	Running against the current of traffic
		Train is divided	Break in two
		Tail lamp	Used instead of marker lamp
Stacking	Coal piles	Dead end bay	Sub station
Yard controllers	Yardmasters		

INDEX

Numbers in italics refer to illustrations.

ACKNOWLEDGEMENTS

The Publisher wishes to thank the following persons for supplying photographs: Australian News & Information Bureau: 94, 110; British Rail: back flap, 15, 16, 18, 23, 27, 53, 54, 57, 99; Canadian Pacific Rail: 105, 114, 150; CCQ (T.B. Owen): 108; CCQ (R.M. Quinn): 109; CCQ (N. Shepherd): 119; John R. Day: 124, 125, 126, 127, 128, 129, 130, 131, 132; Harold Edmondson: rear endpaper, 33, 52; Freightliners Ltd: 157; Victor Hand: front jacket, back jacket, front endpaper, 40, 65, 67, 74, 75, 76, 77, 78, 79, 80, 81, 82, 83, 84, 85, 86, 87, 88, 89, 90, 98, 101, 104, 111, 138, 143, 152, 158; Brian Haresnape: 1, 13, 17, 21, 55, 60, 62; F.R. Hebron: 58, 63; Richard Kindig: 43, 44, 49, 50, 51, 71, 72, 73, 161; Lens of Sutton: 20, 22, 25; Locomotive Publishing Co: 24, 26; London Transport Board: 116, 121, 123; Museum of British Transport: front jacket, title page, 4, 10, 160; Ed Nowak: 32, 66, 68, 69, 70; Radio Times Hulton Picture Library: contents page, 3, 9, 19, 29, 34, 35, 37, 38, 39, 41, 42, 45, 46, 47, 48, 56, 59, 61, 91, 93, 100, 117, 118, 120; Railways of Australia: 148, 155, 156; A.J. Russell: 28; Science Museum: 2, 5, 6, 7, 8, 11, 12, 14, 36; United States Information Service: 30, 31, 64, 122; Peter F. Winding: 95, 96, 97, 102, 103, 106, 107, 112, 113, 115; Ian Yearsley: 133, 134, 135, 136, 137, 139, 140, 141, 142, 144, 145, 146, 147, 149, 151, 153, 154, 159.